ALETHEIA ADVENTU[

RUMOUR MILL

E.M.WILKIE

THE RUMOUR MILL

Aletheia Adventure Series Book 6

Book 3 of the Battle for Aletheia Trilogy

E M Wilkie

JOHN RITCHIE LTD
CHRISTIAN PUBLICATIONS

Copyright © 2016 by John Ritchie Ltd.
40 Beansburn, Kilmarnock, Scotland

www.ritchiechristianmedia.co.uk

ISBN-13: 978 1 910513 56 9

Written by E M Wilkie
Illustrated by E M Wilkie
www.aletheiabooks.co
Copyright © 2016

Cover illustration by Graeme Hewitson.
Interior illustrations are by E M Wilkie.

Unless otherwise indicated, Scripture quotations are taken from:
The Holy Bible, New King James Version®.
© 1982 by Thomas Nelson, Inc. Used by permission. All rights reserved.

Printed by Bell and Bain Ltd, Glasgow.

To my nieces and nephews,
Zach, Bobby, Seth, Harry, Emily, Abigail, Olivia, and Alexander;

And to all the other children who have enjoyed these
adventure stories.

This book was written with the desire,

'That Christ may dwell in your hearts through faith; that
you...may be able to comprehend...what is the width and length
and depth and height – to know the love of Christ which passes
knowledge; that you may be filled with all the fullness of God.'
[Ephesians 3:17-19]

"God is love."
1 John 4:8

"If God so loved us, we also ought to love one another."
1 John 4:11

PREFACE

This story is an attempt to help and encourage young readers to develop an understanding of the truth contained in the Word of God, the Bible. However, all characters, places, descriptions and incidents are entirely fictional and this adventure story is not intended to be a substitute for the teaching contained in the Bible, but rather an aid to understanding. The illustrations and allegories used in this story are not perfect; and therefore, whilst it is hoped that readers will benefit from the truth and lessons developed in this story, they must be urged to develop an understanding of Bible truth and doctrine from the Bible alone.

Once again, the author is indebted to other people who helped, advised and in other ways supported the production of this book. In particular, the assistance of the following people has been invaluable and is greatly appreciated:

M J Wilkie, E Taylor, R Hatt, H Munro, A Henderson, S Jackson, R Chesney, and Margareta.

Many thanks to you all.

CONTENTS

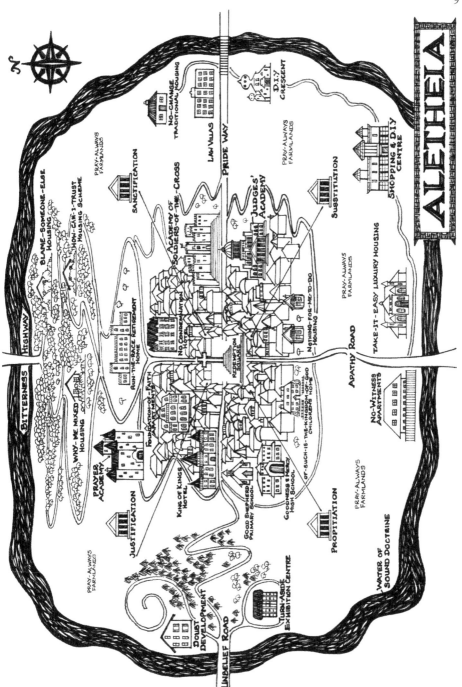

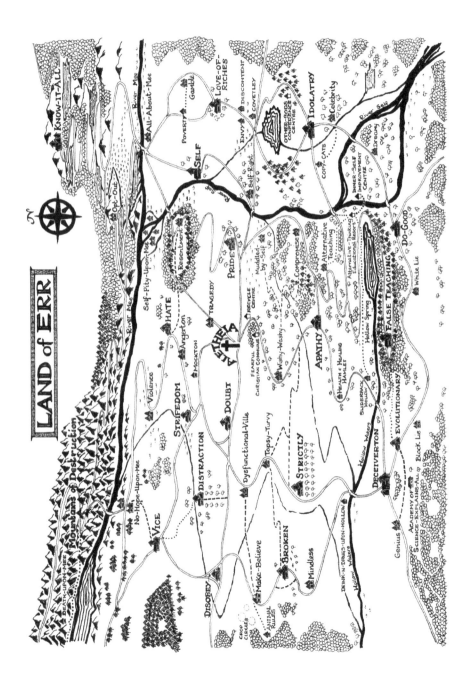

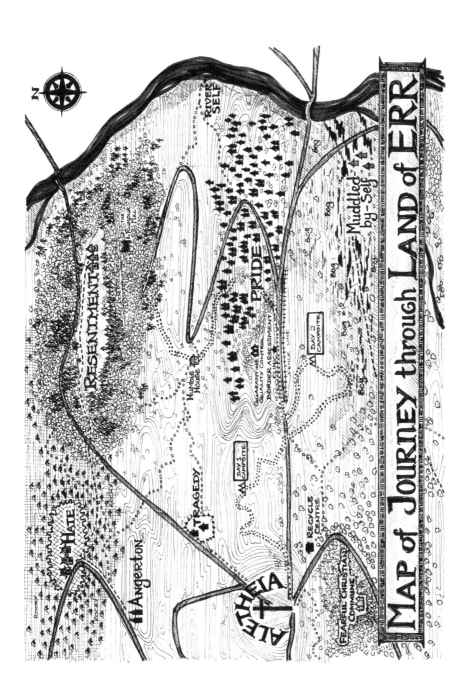

PROLOGUE

Grey mist crept through dripping trees. Shadows brooded. Drizzle fell. Light fled the sky. Evening approached. Soon it would be night.

A twig snapped.

Two women paused, huddled and secretive. When there was silence they walked on through the eerie grounds. Anxiously listening. Unable to see through the cloud and darkness. Once, lighting had been considered for these parklands. But they preferred darkness.

One of the women was Governor Genie, the leader of the land of Err. She was from Region 2, the home of the headquarters of the ruling Council of Err, where they now walked. The other was Lilotta Mostly, the Regional Representative of neighbouring Region 3. The two spoke quietly – planning and scheming. Their breath filled the air with puffs of white vapour. It was chilly, despite being spring.

The women did not like each other, but they were united in one thing: they hated Region 15. This was the city of Aletheia. It stood for Bible Truth and refused to admit any other version of Truth at all. The land of Err called it Region 15.

The Governor's foot slipped unexpectedly and she stumbled. Lilotta expressed polite concern which she didn't feel. Governor Genie stopped and inspected her shoe – on the sole of which was a squashed, slimy, still-wriggling worm. Her lip curled in a sneer. She wished the troublesome city of Aletheia was as easily overcome as this helpless worm. She flicked it from her shoe in disgust and wiped her fingers on a clean handkerchief. She wished she could wipe them on Lilotta's ridiculous, pretentious white coat instead.

"The Rumour Mill?" prompted Lilotta, returning to the matter they had been discussing. "If open invasion didn't bring Region 15 under our control, how will the Rumour Mill?"

The Governor wiped her fingers in her handkerchief once more. She had the uncomfortable feeling she had worm-goo under her fingernails. Quietly, she said, "We let them destroy themselves."

"Through the Rumour Mill? Through the Meddlers?"

"Exactly. The leaders of Aletheia will be so discredited by the Meddlers' rumours that the people of Aletheia will welcome new leaders from the land of Err. As for their *truth* which they hold so precious, soon there will be no truth left. They won't know what to believe! Then they will gladly join with the Council of Err. They will, at last, share our own truths and values!"

"And the White-Jacket Meddlers?" Lilotta asked eagerly.

"They will, as you would expect, play a vital part."

Lilotta began to understand the plan – the plan she was part of because the Governor needed the use of the subtle creatures known as White-Jacket Meddlers: Meddlers that specialised in lies and deceit. Region 3, and the town of White Lie where Lilotta lived, was the natural home of these tricky creatures. The region was famous for its subtle changes to truth, twisting and turning it such that you never knew what was true – and what was not.

Region 3 never admitted to approving of lies, but they did admit that the truth could be many things. In fact, truth could be precisely what you wanted it to be. If the ideas were subtle enough, with just enough truth twisted by exaggeration, with a bit of spice and interest added for good measure, people would believe anything! This plan was certain to succeed.

In the still, misty air they could smell the stench of decay from a rotting animal.

"A dead rabbit, I think," Lilotta remarked carelessly.

Genie didn't answer. Her mind was still on the Meddlers – her best hope to finally overcome the stubborn city of Aletheia. But was she right to pin so much on creatures she knew were intrinsically unreliable? In her mind she saw the tiny, cunning face of a wayward, fickle creature she had come to dread: the leader of the Meddlers.

She had first met him in the Governor's luxurious office – a horrible surprise contained in an old, tatty cupboard she had thought to get rid of. The cupboard looked forgotten and neglected; no one had thought to enquire what was within. It was kept locked, and only the governors of the land of Err were ever initiated into its secrets. It was home to the leader of the Meddlers – a Blue-Stocking Meddler simply called *Sir-Meddle*. The Meddler leader used the insides of walls and ceilings and pipes to get from the outside world into the back of the cupboard. Inside his 'office' he had a tiny desk and a store of smelly food. Sir-Meddle unlocked and opened the cupboard door when he pleased; he demanded what he pleased; stole what he pleased; and it was only when he *was* pleased that he deigned to discuss and advise on the business of the Meddlers in the land of Err. Often Governor Genie wondered who was in control of whom – the Meddlers or the government? Of course, it was far too late to think of doing without the Meddlers; nobody knew how to get rid of them. But almost, *almost* she wished Sir-Meddle was the creature decaying out there beyond the shadows…

Meanwhile, she could only think to direct the Meddlers' many evil deeds against their common enemy:

Against Region 15; against *Aletheia*.

Yes, the Rumour Mill, the terrifying headquarters of the Meddlers, would conquer the Truth of Aletheia.

With lies.

PART 1: THE DISCOVERY

CHAPTER 1
RUMOURS

It was spring once more in Aletheia. The city of Bible Truth, in the centre of the land of Err, was growing and thriving. Across the Pray-Always Farmlands, newly planted trees were blossoming, crops were budding, farmhouses and barns had been freshly painted, and cows were enjoying the first fresh grass of the season. There was little evidence of the occupation and pollution that Aletheia had endured when the land of Err had invaded the city the previous autumn.[1] Signs of the war were nearly gone.

For the children of the city, the end of the war meant the return of all the schoolchildren to Aletheia. School had reopened. Charlie Steady had very mixed feelings about returning to Aletheia and to Goodness and Mercy High School. He had been absent for the duration of the war, sent to stay with relatives in the country of Phronesis – "out of harm's way". Apart from leaving his best friend, Benjamin Wright, Charlie was quite happy to leave the gloom of besieged Aletheia to stay in Phronesis. He craved the danger and adventure he was sure he would find there. But there wasn't much action after all, and Charlie got bored of his aunt and uncle's well-meaning lectures about the Bible and the way of salvation. He got enough of that in Aletheia.

Now that Charlie was back in Aletheia, he discovered a most unwelcome and alarming change. It wasn't change in the city; that didn't concern him. School hadn't changed for the better either; but he had never been optimistic about that. Nor had his family improved in his absence – which he thought was a pity. As far as he was concerned, his Christian relatives were a distinctly hampering influence on his desire for adventure.

But there *was* the most shocking and unwelcome change in his friend, Benjamin Wright. Charlie had always relied upon Ben to share his disapproval of Aletheia; but during the war, Ben had actually changed sides![1] It was a most disheartening development and Charlie was concerned.

"Of course I know what it means to be saved," he said impatiently, when Ben tried to explain what had happened to him – and how he had become a Christian.[2] "That's all anybody in Aletheia cares about! That's *all* we've been taught about *all* our lives!" Charlie never minded exaggerating to make a point.

"Well, now I know *why* they all think it's so important," said Ben. "It's actually *real*, Charlie! It really is!"

"*Real*," repeated Charlie, who always enjoyed a debate. "I suppose there are plenty of important *real* things in the world. Real people, real money, real buildings…"

"That's not what I meant!"

"And they're all *more real* – because you can see them – than something like *being saved* – which you can't see at all!"

Benjamin was usually very good at winning arguments – but if there was one person who was better at it, it was his friend Charlie. Charlie could answer anything – or tie you in knots so that you thought he had.

Ben tried to explain. "It's invisible because it happens *inside* you. But I've been made completely right before God, because of what the Lord Jesus has done! I know I have! And that's *real!*"

"Well, as long as it doesn't mean you go all boring and good," remarked Charlie. "I never thought *you* would be like this, Ben! I thought we would always stick together!"

Benjamin went a bit red. "Of course I'm not boring!"

"I expect *Aunt Sagacia* thinks you'll make a great, *boring* Judge," said Charlie. He grinned when Ben went red again. That Ben was actually interested in the Judges' Academy, was another amazing thing which had happened while Charlie had been away. Charlie's aunt was Sagacia Steady, the Chief Judge of Aletheia. Ben had helped her to solve some problem or other,[1] and now he spent most of his free time helping Justice Jude Faithful, doing goodness knows what – reading boring, musty manuscripts for all Charlie knew. Nor was he pleased with the strange new friends Ben hung around with: like Flair Scholar – the annoying know-it-all from their class at school, and Dusty Addle – nice enough, but a bit of a nutty professor.

"But I *would* like to have seen a Meddler," Charlie mused, as he and Ben continued walking home from school, discussing what had happened during the war. "There are none left in Aletheia now, I suppose?"

"None," said Ben. "But what I'm helping Jude Faithful with, *is* about Meddlers!"

Charlie ignored that. He refused to be interested in whatever Ben did at the Judges' Academy. "I wonder what action there might be around here, now that the invasion's over and Aletheia's back to normal." Charlie scanned the peaceful, prosperous surroundings disdainfully.

Ben said nothing. He didn't think he could adequately explain to Charlie how awful the invasion had been – and how wonderful it was that the city was now restored.

"And what's this old Whiskers is talking about – that our topic this term is about love in the Bible?!" 'Whiskers' was the students' nickname for their formidable Headmaster and Head of Education, Mr Philologus Mustardpot.

"I wonder if it's to do with the Rumour Mill," said Ben.

Charlie stared at his friend. "The *Rumour Mill?!*" he echoed incredulously.

Benjamin shuffled uncomfortably. Should he be talking about this? Was it meant to be a secret that the Meddlers had their headquarters at the mysterious Rumour Mill? "Don't tell anyone, but it's to do with what I'm helping Jude Faithful with," he explained. "The Meddlers might be close by the city, ready to start trouble again."

"What kind of trouble?" asked Charlie eagerly. "Another fight? Or blight on the crops? Or…"

Ben shook his head. "Nothing like that. It's to do with spreading lies about the Truth of the Bible, and about all the important people of Aletheia too."

"Why would Meddlers bother with the leaders of Aletheia?" Charlie was bored again. "I wouldn't have thought there was much to say about *them!*" Personally he couldn't imagine anything less interesting than the mundane, immaculate lives of the busy managers of Aletheia. "Anyway, I don't see how spreading *rumours* about the *managers* will make much difference!"

"But, the point is, perhaps that's why Whiskers is making us learn about love in the Bible," said Ben.

Charlie had lost track. He didn't see the link at all. In any case, he didn't think something as wishy-washy as *love* would fend off Meddlers.

Instead, he contemplated with interest the possibility that the small, pesky Meddlers were close to Aletheia once more. Perhaps, if he was lucky, they would provide some action, after all!

The following day was Saturday – a precious free day away from school. Charlie left an apologetic Ben at the Judges' Academy. He refused to join Ben and see what he and Jude Faithful were studying, despite Ben's promise that it was "really very interesting". Charlie didn't think anything that involved the Judges' Academy, Flair Scholar and Dusty Addle, was likely to prove even slightly interesting, let alone *very* interesting!

He took himself off across the pleasant farmlands, down the sloping fields to the boundary of Aletheia. He went by way of Apathy Road because it was the easiest route, and examined with interest the nearly-deserted luxury homes at Take-It-Easy Luxury Housing. All but one were boarded up. He wondered, not for the first time, why his parents weren't go-ahead enough to move into one of the empty houses; but he knew they would not.

In the one occupied house, a man in a silk, patterned dressing gown was walking down an immaculate, paved path, admiring his flower beds. He looked up as he heard Charlie approach and almost dropped his mug of steaming coffee in surprise.

"Have you just got out of bed?" asked Charlie.

The man frowned. He suspected Charlie was being cheeky. "I'll have you know I work very hard all week!" he snapped.

Charlie nodded. "Me too," he said, thinking of school and all the homework he had yet to do. But he had left that behind unfinished. He felt that Saturdays were *never* meant for schoolwork. "Are you very rich?" he continued with interest.

The man gave a short laugh. "That's none of your business!"

"Well, it's certainly more your business than mine," agreed Charlie, "but that doesn't mean that it's *none* of mine, does it? I mean, it could be a *tiny* bit of my business, couldn't it? Because… well, what if I wanted to work for you, for example, or copy what you did to make loads of money?"

The man had not come across a boy like Charlie before – who had an answer for everything. He stared at him for a moment in silence, so Charlie continued, "Where are all the other people who used to live here?"

"They've gone back to the centre of Aletheia, back to the cross." The man retreated a step towards the house.

"Why?"

"You should ask them that!" He took another step away from Charlie.

"Well, I can't, can I?" said Charlie reasonably. "I mean, how can I ask them anything at all, if I don't know them, and don't know where they're living, or their names or anything? But since *you* knew them, I thought *you* might have asked them why they left their nice houses and moved. In fact, *you* were probably there *when* they moved. You might even have helped to carry their boxes and cases, you know, like neighbours do for each other. Just helping..." Charlie trailed off. Sometimes he got lost in his own arguments and couldn't remember the original point.

The man wasn't about to tell this boy that he had watched all his neighbours move back to the cross from his upstairs window. He *was* about to tell Charlie it was none of his business when he remembered that answer hadn't got him anywhere before.

"I don't know why they went," he said shortly. "They said they needed to live near the cross, but I don't think it's as nice or easy there."

"No," agreed Charlie fervently, surveying the beautiful private garden. "You must be lonely here now," he added.

"It's usually very *peaceful*," the man said pointedly.

Charlie didn't recognise subtle hints. "That's a good way of looking at it! I'd quite like a nice big house all on my own too. Well, I'd better be on my way. If I'm passing this way again I'll come and see how you are! Maybe you'll have new neighbours soon. I wish my family would move here!" He gave a cheerful wave, and the utterly bemused man watched him walk away.

Charlie was puzzled for different reasons. Very strange and curious things had happened since the invasion of Aletheia. What made people once living in luxury move back to the centre of the city, near the cross? It made no sense!

He walked on, to the boundary of Aletheia.

Without a backward glance, he stepped into the land of Err.

Charlie went as far as the Recycle Centre on Apathy Road, not far outside the city. Often in the past, he and Ben enjoyed a chat with Bob, the friendly man who ran the Recycle Centre and bought and sold and exchanged books and plenty of other things too. Bob picked up all the gossip about the land of Err and the city of Aletheia; he knew everything that was going on.

Bob was pleased to see him. Business was slow, despite the fact the sun was shining and it was Saturday morning, usually his busiest time. But there were only a few people about, and they were mostly poking through the early lettuce and spring onions someone was selling on a makeshift stall close by.

"Things have been slow around here since the folk from Err left Aletheia," explained Bob. "Now, hardly anyone in Aletheia wants to exchange their Bible for anything else!"

Charlie took his accustomed seat in a tatty deck chair, by the outdoor 'bargain' tables.

"Anyway, I thought you'd gone away for good!" Bob settled back in his own deck chair and closed his eyes to enjoy a spot of sunbathing while they talked.

"My folks thought I should be away, you know, for the war." Charlie didn't explain that they thought he could cause less trouble if he was absent.

"War?" echoed Bob. "Is *that* what they're calling it?"

Charlie shrugged. "Well, the invasion then."

Bob managed to look dubious, even with his eyes shut and half asleep. "If you ask me, that's just what the *leaders* in Aletheia *want* you to believe. I heard it was to do with pollution in the city, that's all!"

"What do you mean?" asked Charlie. He took a bite from the big slice of chocolate cake that Bob had produced.

"I wonder... well, maybe I shouldn't repeat it." Bob enjoyed being mysterious and Charlie knew that, given time, he would tell all.

He took another big bite of the chocolate cake. It was sweeter than the cakes in Aletheia, but it never truly satisfied hunger. "Have you heard things about the leaders of Aletheia?" he prompted, fearing Bob had fallen asleep.

Bob spoke ponderously. "Maybe. I mean, you ask yourself why the Chief of Aletheia thinks the city was *invaded*, and yet all the findings are that it suffered from acid pollution!"

"Acid pollution!" exclaimed Charlie in disbelief. In his mind he could see the healthy, thriving crops of the Pray-Always Farmlands and the clean, repaired city. It certainly didn't look like Aletheia had been polluted by acid!

"Well, they've got you convinced anyway," grunted Bob, opening one eye to see Charlie.

Charlie shifted uncomfortably. "I don't know about that," he muttered. "But if there was acid pollution…" He was still thinking about the green crops.

Bob grew confiding. "They're saying that not only did the Chief cover up the acid pollution and move all the people back aboveground into the dangerous pollution, but he *bribed* all the officials of Err to leave Aletheia – and then he claimed the victory! So there was no war after all!"

Charlie suddenly lost interest in the chocolate cake. Had the Chief really paid money or treasure to the government of Err to make them leave the city? Was *that* how the so-called war ended? Charlie wasn't afraid of holding a firm opinion on just about everything; but right now he was baffled.

Bob continued, "Mind you, I'm not saying that's what *I* believe," he said, "I'm only telling you what *other people* are saying, people that know more than you and me do about the situation…"

Bob went on talking, and Charlie suddenly remembered. What was it Ben had said about the Meddlers? It was to do with lies about the leaders of Aletheia. Bob chatted on, and Charlie listened to the rumours.

He wondered what it all meant.

CHAPTER 2
TEAM MEDDLER

Dusty Addle walked jauntily through the sunshine of Aletheia. He had just left the fantastic complexity of the Central Control Room at the Academy of Soldiers-of-the-Cross, where he spent all his spare hours helping with the work there. With him walked an untidy girl, who occasionally broke into an impromptu run to keep up with her long-legged companion. The girl had large, smeared glasses, and an oversized, scruffy leather satchel slung about her. It bumped and jolted as she rushed after Dusty through the paved streets of Aletheia, towards the immaculate splendour of the Judges' Academy.

"It's not a race, you know, Dusty," she protested. "We'll only be a matter of seconds later with our news if we walk a little slower!"

"Sorry," said the good-humoured Dusty. He accommodated her slower stride for a couple of steps, and then began to hurry again without thinking. He was anxious, as she was, to share the news of their latest research.

Dusty whistled as he walked, for the sun was shining, the majestic buildings of central Aletheia were gleaming, and everywhere there was evidence of the victory and cleansing of the city of Truth. Flair

Scholar, his companion, hoisted her heavy satchel of books into her arms and tried to keep pace.

"I can tell you exactly how many seconds' difference it would take us to reach the Judges' Academy if we walked at approximately half the pace," she panted. "If speed equals distance divided by time, then…"

Dusty wasn't listening and Flair did not have enough breath to explain something that Dusty, who was equally scientific, knew very well anyway. For once, Flair began to wish she had left her satchel of precious books and documents behind.

Dusty didn't carry a bag of books. He clutched a neat folder in his hand. It had been a point of discussion between Dusty and Flair who would carry the precious reports, but Dusty had settled that by pointing at Flair's cumbersome luggage, and refused to let her put the important information they carried in amongst her jumbled possessions.

When they reached the spotless corridors of the Judges' domain, Dusty stopped whistling and slowed his pace. Even Dusty was not immune to the subduing effect of the corridors of the majestic Judges' Academy. Flair sighed with relief. It was cool and quiet here. They made their way to Justice Jude Faithful's room.

There was no need to knock on the door: they were expected and it was open. Jude was seated at his desk. Benjamin was hovering at another table, painstakingly spreading a large, ancient, detailed map across it – placing small weights around the edges that were inclined to curl up again and again without any encouragement.

"It's been so long since we studied that map that it doesn't want to lie flat," Jude observed, watching Ben wrestling with the large document. "The area around Fearful Christian Commune hasn't been examined in any detail for years."

"It has been examined by me," said Ben. "Charlie and I used to go and explore and spy on the weirdos there!"

Jude didn't get a chance to respond to this. That was when Flair and Dusty walked in.

"Hey!" said Ben, holding the map down with one hand as he greeted the entrance of Dusty and Flair. "Now *Team Meddler* is together again!"

The four of them – the newly promoted Justice Jude Faithful, who was their boss and team leader, and the three students, Dusty Addle, Flair Scholar, and Benjamin Wright – made up the small team who had been commissioned to examine Meddler activity around the boundaries of Aletheia. With very few exceptions, none of the managers of Aletheia thought they would find much. But the team took their work very seriously: they worked all the spare hours they could, researching and examining evidence, and relying on the expertise of Dusty and Flair who worked in the Central Control Room at the Academy of Soldiers-of-the-Cross.

This group was one of many that were now researching creatures, inventions, patterns, and reports from across the land of Err, hoping to discover more about their enemies' next plans to attack the city. Every possibility, however unlikely, must be explored.

Dusty joined Ben at the map. "I've got the report," he said without preamble.

"Did we find them?" asked Ben eagerly.

Dusty gave a nod, accompanied by a wide grin.

Flair dumped her large satchel on the ground and said, "Just wait until you see!"

Jude watched the three of them, wondering what they would find next. There was never a dull moment with these three classmates. Although not many would swap places with him, he was glad he had been chosen to work with such clever, interesting students.

Ben searched the cluttered space for another object to keep the map in place. He eyed Flair's satchel which he knew contained plenty of books, but it was inconveniently out of reach. In the end he removed his shoe and plonked it on the last remaining corner, pleased that the map was secured at last.

 Jude chose to overlook the small amount of mud now stuck to an ancient, valuable map belonging to the Judges' Academy. It was one of those things that came with working with Ben Wright. He hoped the Chief Judge – who was so supportive of their project and was one of the few who thought they might find something of interest – did not choose that moment to appear.

"Let's see the report, Dusty," said Jude. He got up from his desk and joined the two boys and Flair at the table. "What does it show today?"

Ben wished Charlie would take an interest in these developments in the search for the Meddlers, especially if they had *found them*! If only Charlie would listen for long enough, he was certain his friend would enjoy learning about Meddlers as much as he had done. Although, he might have plenty of scathing comments about spending time with the eccentric Dusty Addle, and especially with the school know-it-all, Flair Scholar.

Jude spread out Dusty's report which showed the results of a detailed examination of the Rascal Register. The Register had searched extensively for Meddler activity close to the boundaries of

Aletheia, in the same area shown on the ancient map now pinned down with the assistance of Ben's shoe.

"As you know, we've been searching for Blue-Stocking Meddlers for weeks," said Dusty.

"The cleverest Meddlers!" Ben enjoyed making frequent observations on everything he knew about. "But we didn't find any of them close by, did we?"

"No, of course not," said Flair.

"There are still none showing," added Dusty.

Jude was frowning at the curious squiggles on the report. "So, what is this pattern here, then?"

Flair rubbed her hands together and Dusty grinned. "Well, Ben was looking at other types of Meddlers, those likely to be used for this sort of attack. You know, Meddlers that would be useful to spread lies and wrong information. We didn't want to tell you until we'd checked it out."

Ben nodded. "I asked them to search for White-Jacket Meddlers," he said. "Did you find them?"

"All in good time," said Flair, looking smug.

Ben sighed. Flair was generally alright to work with, even if he didn't consider her exactly *normal*, but she could still be an annoying kind of girl.

"White-Jacket Meddlers are very rare in this area," Jude remarked cautiously. "They generally prefer the southern climate of White Lie in Region 3, and the company of academics such as those who work at the Academy of Science-Explains-All. Because they specialise in lies, they hate coming anywhere near the source of the Truth. They don't usually survive up here. They can't breathe the air."

"Which means they wouldn't be suspected of being up here, would they? But they're the very ones that like twisting truth into lies!" said Ben.

"And the pattern on this report…"

"It's White-Jacket Meddlers, isn't it?!" cried Ben triumphantly.

"They're there alright," said Flair happily.

Jude bent over the large map, astonished and not yet sure what to believe. He picked up some small coloured flags. "It's hard to see the exact vicinity from the report, but I would guess within this area here…" Jude laid out the coloured flags around an area outside the southern boundary of Aletheia – which included the Recycle Centre and Fearful Christian Commune. "But, even so, one of the things about White-Jacket Meddlers is that they are so tricky they could make it appear that they're somewhere that they're not…"

Dusty cleared his throat. "Um, there's something else."

"Tell them!" exclaimed Flair, clearly wanting to do just that.

With a curious mix of triumph and abject sheepishness, Dusty removed a second report from his pocket.

"Go, Dusty!" exclaimed Ben, thumping him on the back.

"Actually, this one was Flair's idea."

Flair nodded, looking pleased. "But Dusty and I worked on it together," she said generously.

Dusty looked hesitant – even guilty. "Uh, we didn't exactly have direct permission to run this report."

"Jude, um, I mean, *Justice Faithful* says we can do what we want in our research," said Ben.

"I can't remember saying anything quite as drastic and far reaching," remarked Jude drily. "But I'm sure you and Flair acted within your remit, Dusty," he added.

Reluctantly, Dusty admitted, "Well, it didn't go completely right."

"Not right at all," echoed Flair.

"Tell us about the report, and then we'll deal with the problems," suggested Jude. He had reasonable confidence in Dusty's abilities, and Flair had proved more-or-less sensible...

"We ran a report from the Weather Guide," Dusty explained.

Flair gave a nervous giggle. "Only, the Weather Guide didn't seem to like it very much!"

"We followed the information from the first report, from the Rascal

Register, and asked it to track weather signals in the same area and at the same time as the White-Jacket Meddlers have been showing outside Aletheia."

"Well, I never," muttered Jude.

Ben exclaimed, "Weather! I never thought of that!"

"We knew that sometimes the weather changes when there are problems in Err, and we thought the White-Jacket Meddlers might be linked with local weather anomalies…"

"Yes, well?" prompted Jude.

At last Dusty opened the second, secret report. The report made no real sense to Ben, or even Jude, and, in addition, it was *damp*. "White mist and cloud is the key," said Dusty. "The type of mist you get on a sunny day, early in the morning; the type of fluffy white clouds you get on nice days…"

"Even off-white smoke-like clouds you might expect from a bonfire!" said Flair.

"Really?" Ben was intrigued, but not surprised, that his friends had found something. He expected groundbreaking discoveries all the time.

"You *actually found* a link between *weather and Meddlers?*" asked Jude, astounded. "So, where there is an accumulation of white cloud, smoke, or mist…"

"That's when the White-Jackets are active," said Dusty. "I think it probably vanishes when they're at rest or not planning, but where there are lots of them congregating and busy…"

"Then there are clouds!" exclaimed Flair. "No doubt about it!"

"They emit white vapour," said Jude, talking to himself. "White Lie, in the land of Err, and that whole area, is notoriously cloudy and misty; it clouds all of the issues, you see…"

"Not really," said Ben frankly, "but well done, Dusty and Flair! *Team Meddler* is going to beat all the other teams!"

"It's not a competition," mumbled Jude, bending over the map and considering what Dusty had just divulged. "So if we watch, track, observe white mist in these areas…"

"It *might* lead us straight to the White-Jacket Meddlers," agreed Dusty.

"Who are otherwise notoriously difficult to find," completed Jude. "They're so very good at disguise and subtlety. Well done! Very well done!"

"But about the problem because of our research with the Weather Guide…"

Jude was distracted, thinking about this latest information and all its sudden possibilities. "Yes? Whatever it is, I'll sort it. This might be essential information…"

Flair gave another inadvertent giggle. "You might need to explain that bit to Mr Buffer!"

Mr Brian Buffer was the Central Control Room Manager, with whom Dusty and Flair were usually on good terms.

"The Weather Guide got a bit carried away pumping out white vapour," Dusty explained desperately.

"And no one is quite sure how to stop it!" added Flair, sounding very amused.

Ben was astonished. Until now, he hadn't thought Flair had a sense of humour.

"I suppose this explains the damp report," said Jude drily.

"Well, *everything* is a bit damp, and the mist is now so dense no one can see to work!" concluded Dusty.

Jude grimaced. "I think you well named us *Team Meddler*, Ben. Soon others will be calling us that too! I think I'd better come and explain to Mr Buffer."

But, no matter what problems there now were in the Control Room as a result of their overzealous research, Justice Faithful had the first glimmerings of hope that his unique team might, after all, help to locate the enemy of Aletheia.

CHAPTER 3
APPROVAL

Behind thick stone walls, deep inside the impenetrable fortress which was the Academy of Soldiers-of-the-Cross, a group of important people gathered in a large room, around a massive table. There were men and women in uniform with medals; others in smart suits and crisp shirts; the Chief Judge, Sagacia Steady, in her impressive, flowing robe; and Mr Croft Straw, the Pray-Always Farmlands Representative, in his pressed tweed suit and best tie – which had images of black and white cows all over it. These were the managers, heads, directors, and chiefs of all the different departments in Aletheia. They met to plan the defence of the city Aletheia – against the next attack of the Council of Err.

Exactly how and when the next attack might come they did not know. A small number were sure this would once more be directed by the troublesome and wicked Meddlers, through whom they had already suffered so much. Others felt that, since the Council of Err had already used Meddlers and been defeated twice, this time the attack would come by other means.

Chief Robert Steadfast had ultimate responsibility for safeguarding the city of Bible Truth from another attack by its enemies. He was determined they would investigate *all* possibilities. And now the leaders of Aletheia were meeting to update the Chief on the progress of their teams of busy staff who analysed every development in the land of Err which might cause yet more harm to their beloved city. The Chief and his advisors listened to the latest reports by the various teams.

A bespectacled man was speaking from the front of the room. He was a senior technician, a long way down the chain from the clever Chief Scientist of Aletheia and Director of Health, Dr Theo Pentone – who was in charge of all scientific and medical activity in Aletheia. "Our information is that Deceivedors have been the subject of further studies and experiments at the Academy of Science-Explains-All," said the technician.

"What is the implication for Aletheia?" asked Captain Ready Steadfast. He was the son of the Chief, and also the Deputy Chief of Aletheia.

"Potentially, it means that the Deceivedors will become a massive army of almost indestructible force – that will openly attack and assault Aletheia."

Dr Pentone stifled a yawn. He tried not to let it show to the senior technician, who was only doing his job. They had been instructed to investigate even the unlikely. But that did mean that many of the reports were, in the doctor's opinion, just that: extremely unlikely.

"Doctor Pentone?" Captain Steadfast's sharp eyes were upon him. "Theo, are you concerned at the further development of the Deceivedors? We know the Council of Err were unsuccessful in using them against us last autumn;[1] do you consider them to be a significant threat now?"

Dr Pentone sat up straighter and tried to smooth his ever-rumpled lab coat. "I don't think this should be our primary area of concern, Captain," he said. "As instructed, we are exploring *every* avenue of possibility, however unlikely. The further development of the Deceivedors is, of course, deplorable. They are disgusting creatures! But I don't believe the next attack will be such an obvious assault. They must know that they would fail to cross our boundaries since the Water of Sound Doctrine is restored. Even a huge army of monsters will falter before the Water of Sound Doctrine!"

The further reports from Dr Pentone's staff included the development of a new gas-like substance which sent people to sleep for several days. The doctor speeded up the explanation the keen lab technician had prepared which related to creatures known as Sloths. "Stick to the main point," he said kindly. "In theory, the substance could potentially be dropped on the city and send us all to sleep – assuming, of course, we have all lost our minds in the meantime and stopped praying and preparing and defending ourselves!"

The lab technician sat down and the next expert stood up and gave a more concise report on the forging of ancient documents. These purported to contradict the teaching of the Bible: they could undermine people's faith in the reliability of the Word of God.

When the reports from Dr Pentone's staff had ended, the Chief Judge rose to her feet. "I have several updates from my teams, but first I will deal with the one I consider most intriguing." She indicated Jude Faithful. "Justice Faithful, here, is responsible for searching for Meddler activity within a ten mile radius of the city of Aletheia."

There wasn't any special interest in the work of Jude's team. They were hardly noteworthy among so many others, and Jude was well aware that most thought it extremely unlikely the Meddlers could get within ten miles of the city since their thorough defeat last autumn; none of the regular surveillance reports showed up anything of particular concern. Only a few, such as the Chief Judge, thought the Meddlers might find a way to meddle once more.

"Justice Faithful's group have been investigating ways of extracting other details from our Control Room regarding the movements of Meddlers close to the city. I believe they have found something of interest."

Dr Pentone leaned forward, interested in this development. As

Chief Scientist of Aletheia, he knew plenty about the fantastic machines of the Central Control Room. He was never surprised when they yielded something new: they really were the most extraordinary devices.

Jude stood up to give his report. "We have evidence which leads us to suspect that White-Jacket Meddlers are accumulating within a ten mile radius, to the south, south-east, and south-west of our boundary."

Theo Pentone whistled under his breath, enjoying the effect the startling revelation had on the assembled company. How could this be? They had been completely banished in the war!

"Are you certain?" asked the Chief, understandably doubtful. "You're working with a group of students I think, Faithful? White-Jacket Meddlers are notoriously tricky creatures. They can be very deceptive – lies and disguise are their nature of course. They can even appear to be where they are not."

Captain Steadfast added, "We know White-Jacket Meddlers struggle to even come close to our city. They cannot survive near to those who love the Truth; it suffocates them; they cannot live in such pure air. They breathe the poison of lies and delusions. Have you any theories as to how these creatures could possibly be near our boundaries?"

Jude knew this was one of the weakest points in their case. "No, sir," he admitted.

Dr Pentone cleared his throat. "If I may…"

Chief Steadfast waved his hand in assent. "By all means, Theo!"

"I wonder if the answer might be found in a curious, and unforeseen, effect of the war. We know that many of the people living on The Outskirts of our city sadly left Aletheia during the war and settled in the land of Err. They most likely settled close to our boundaries. So, it's possible that there is a significant increase in the number of people who are confused about the Truth, or even believing lies, now living close to our boundaries. This influence might be enough to disguise the tricky White-Jacket Meddlers, and give them sufficient muddled air to breathe. It's only a theory, but…"

"But one which might fit the picture," agreed Captain Steadfast cautiously.

"I am satisfied Justice Faithful and his team have discovered something that is at least worth further investigation," said the Chief Judge.

"Proceed as you see fit, Sagacia," directed the Chief.

"If you need to go on a mission in Err, liaise with Lieutenant Bourne Faithful," added Captain Steadfast. "I'll give him instructions, and he will coordinate anything that you need."

Jude sighed with relief. They had received approval to proceed. He would even be working with his own brother, Bourne. Jude and his small, peculiar team would take the next step in their investigation of the enemies of Aletheia.

The four members of *Team Meddler* were together in Jude's study. The large map was once more set out on the table, and the four of them scrutinised the cluster of carefully placed flags, which marked the area where they thought the White-Jacket Meddlers had been detected.

Ben remarked, "If I were a Meddler, I'd know exactly where to hide!"

"Imagine being able to think like a Meddler!" said Flair.

"Where would you hide?" Jude peered closer at the map. There was plenty of cover and vegetation in the locality. Outside the southern boundary of the city was a region characterised by fear and delusion and confusion about the Truth. It was always an area that was hiding from something.

Ben placed a finger on the map – on the cluster of buildings which were isolated, as an island, in the centre of a jungle of vegetation. "I'd hide right here."

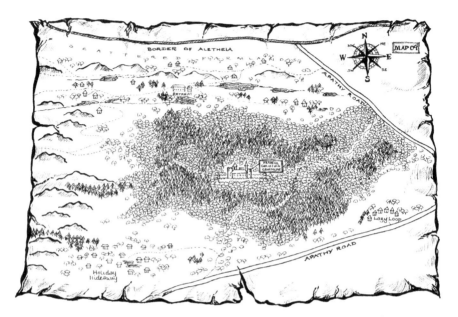

"Fearful Christian Commune," said Flair, reading the name attached to the buildings. "What is that place anyway? I've never seen any activity around there from the Control Room."

"That's the point," said Dusty. "The people there are hidden away from the land of Err and Aletheia because they *don't want* any activity."

"They're afraid the end of the world is coming," said Ben matter-of-factly. "Of course, they're all totally nuts. Charlie and I used to go and spy on them."

"Did you?" Jude enjoyed Benjamin's revelations about his past adventures.

"Imagine that!" exclaimed Flair. She took Ben seriously – which Ben encouraged, interested to see just how gullible Flair could be.

Ben continued, "The folk at the Commune hide if they see or hear anything remotely strange – so they would never interfere with the Meddlers. The Meddlers could hold their annual Christmas party there, and they would all hide in their Commune and think the end of the world had come at last!"

"So, the Meddlers actually have an annual Christmas party…" began Flair.

Before Ben could invent the details of the supposed Meddler party, about which he knew nothing, Jude remarked, "We have little detailed information of the layout of the place. They're so reluctant to invite visitors or accept help of any kind. We visit strictly by invitation. It's an unwritten rule."

"They're nuts, that's why," repeated Ben.

At that moment, Lieutenant Bourne Faithful entered the room. Bourne was a fierce and capable warrior of growing importance in Aletheia. He was revered by the youth of Aletheia – among whom he had attained the status of hero, not least because of the mysterious scar he bore on his face. Accompanying Bourne was his young assistant, Henrietta Wallop, and her twin brother, Hugo. They were in the same class at school as Ben, Dusty, and Flair. Ben was delighted at the growing membership of *Team Meddler*.

Bourne spoke without preamble. "We leave at dawn on Saturday morning. The weather forecast is favourable; we might even catch a glimpse of the white mist Dusty and Flair are so keen on." His eyes were twinkling at his eager audience of students. "We start with the area surrounding Fearful Christian Commune."

CHAPTER 4
SECRET MISSION

The last star of the night was fading from the lightening sky when the group of five walked out of the still sleeping city of Aletheia, down the gently sloping Apathy Road, and into the land of Err. Mist lay silently in the streets of the old city and slowly crept over the Pray-Always Farmlands. It was the type of mist the sun would enjoy burning up later in the morning; it promised to be another glorious spring day. Over the distant Fearful Christian Commune, the mist was impenetrably thick. But this was no indication that the White-Jacket Meddlers were active: the mist was simply everywhere.

Lieutenant Bourne Faithful and Justice Jude Faithful led the small group. Behind them walked Hugo and Henrietta and Ben. They tried not to act too excitedly or speak too loudly. The importance, and secrecy, of their mission had been drilled into them very thoroughly by Bourne. They felt like the most important people in Aletheia; it was as good as being in the secret service! Ben considered the only thing missing from this grand adventure was his friend, Charlie. But Ben had been forbidden to tell him anything about it.

They reached the overgrown, barely discernible entrance to Fearful Christian Commune and all stopped in a huddle. Bourne rummaged in one of the leather bags slung over his shoulder. "Before we go any further…" He handed each of them a Silent Speaker set. They had been instructed to expect a device which they must wear, so the three teenagers tried not to seem too surprised or look like novices who didn't have a clue what they were doing: even if that was the truth of the matter.

Silent Speakers were clever, curious inventions – recently developed by scientists at the Academy of Soldiers-of-the-Cross. Each set consisted of a pair of almost invisible ear plugs which wheedled and tickled their way inside the wearer's ears, like living insects. Tiny wires came from the plugs inside the ears, down the side of the face, and linked onto a small mask which covered the mouth. The mouthpiece was the weirdest bit: it made the wearer look like an alien. It completely swallowed the sound of a voice, and put it into the earpieces of everyone who was linked to the Silent Speakers. There was a tiny switch, just behind the ear. This had a number of channels for different uses. It was most peculiar not being able to hear your own voice except through your earpiece. It was very odd to speak out loud – and yet be utterly silent.

"When we're on channel two, all five of us are connected. Whatever you say, we all hear. Channel three means it's just the three of you connected. Dusty and Flair are linked to both channels and can hear everything. Keep yourselves programmed to channel two until I say otherwise. And since we need to concentrate, we might be better without a running commentary throughout our entire expedition, Ben." Bourne concluded his instructions.

"Right, sir!" said Ben.

Henrietta giggled.

Hugo remarked, "It's a shame there's not a whole suit to make us completely invisible and silent."

"Actually, the Academy is in the process of inventing a *Silent Suit!*" Bourne's voice echoed in their ear pieces. "They're hoping that one day we can go on secret missions and not be heard at all!"

Ben was most intrigued with this idea. "So if you step on a twig, or trip over…"

"The Silent Suit swallows up sounds," agreed Bourne.

"Wow!" Ben enjoyed the way his voice echoed weirdly in his earpiece. He wished he could try whistling or shouting, but he didn't think that would be appreciated by either Bourne or Jude. He thought how cool it would be to creep up on people in a Silent Suit. What fun he and Charlie could have at the Fearful Christian Commune!

Bourne held back a thick creeper and they all walked onto a narrow path. They walked single file without encountering the slightest evidence that anyone or anything was about. Once or twice

Hugo thought he detected the eerie shadow of a Snare fleeing from their path. Snares were frightening shadow creatures, but they would not want to remain where Christians were wearing their armour of God with their Bibles at their sides. The armour of God protected Christians against the enemies that they faced, and the Word of God, was the most important weapon any Christian could ever have.[3]

Occasionally the dewy grass and long weeds tugged at their feet and slowed them down. Creatures called Stumbles were carpeting the path, but they could not withstand the armour boots[3] the group wore, and one glimpse of the light of the Bible sent them fleeing from the track with angry, muffled squeaks.

Over the trees and bushes, and clustered densely over the Commune buildings in the middle of the forest, were clouds of Sloths. It was hard to tell a Sloth from ordinary mist or cloud, but you certainly knew once you entered their territory. Minds became weary and eyelids heavy; sleep became the greatest longing. Of course, a Christian wearing the helmet of salvation was safe from the effect of Sloths. This was the first time Ben had visited the area of Fearful Christian Commune wearing his helmet of salvation. He was amazed that the weird heaviness, which had always been part of exploring this strange place, had gone.

The narrow path between thick, tangled hedges gave way to a

dark, eerie forest where the mist curled curiously around the trees. At last they reached the high stone walls of the Commune. They were not there as visitors today; no one in the Commune knew that a small party of Aletheians was outside their walls with an array of extremely curious equipment.

Bourne found a small clearing in the trees, screened by brambles and wickedly sharp thorns. There was no sound. No birds sang, no woodland animals moved, and there was no sight or sound of a Meddler.

They all put down the pieces of equipment they were carrying and Bourne and Jude worked on assembling the Listening Device: fitting wires together, threading silver thread, twiddling dials, and flicking switches. Hugo handed them things and pretended he knew what he was doing; Henrietta tried to look useful; Ben waited impatiently, anxious for the action to start.

Once the Listening Device was assembled, Jude made contact with Dusty and Flair in the Control Room. These two remaining members of *Team Meddler* had a corner of the Control Room that they had claimed as their own for the duration of the expedition. On a table in front of them, there was a curious-looking instrument – a Listening Device which was identical to the one Bourne had just placed in a hidden patch of forest. Flair flicked a switch and a light immediately glowed bright green.

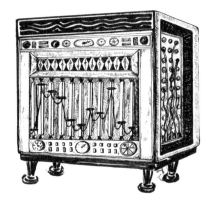

"We're on! It works!" said Flair excitedly.

"Linked to you now, sir, and recording," said Dusty to Jude.

"Received." Jude's voice came through their earpieces.

Dusty and Flair took their seats at the table, their eyes fixed on the curious dials and needles of the Listening Device. One or both of them would remain there for however long it took, hoping to record the plans of the Meddlers.

In the hideout Bourne had chosen, the dense, unfriendly mist continued to curl its chilly tendrils around them. Now that the link with the Control Room had been established, the small team were ready to search for and record any possible sound of the Meddlers. Dusty and Flair's latest report of Meddler presence was unfortunately vague. It was a very slender chance they would find anything at all.

"All we can see is that the mist is thickest at the centre, over the Commune itself," said Dusty.

Bourne sighed. "Which is exactly where we can't reach, unless we alert the folks at the Commune that we're here!"

"Um, not to contradict you, sir, but there *is* a secret way into the Commune," said Ben.

Jude asked drily, "And is it safe and discreet?"

"Yeah," said Ben. "Charlie and I used to spy on them, remember? There's a secret way under the wall – probably made by one of the nutters in the past. Although, it's more animal size, not really for adults. But it was quite overgrown when we found it, so I don't think it's been used recently, which means they probably don't remember about it now, you see?" This was a more optimistic than accurate assessment: the grubby tunnel had appeared unused, and Ben simply hoped it remained that way.

Bourne thought for a moment. Then he made a decision. Missions were seldom without risks, and it was unlikely that he and Jude could fit through the 'animal size' tunnel of Ben's description. So, he must trust the teenagers. "Ben, you, Henry and Hugo explore this tunnel and the Commune grounds if you get into them. Be discreet, and finish before any of the Commune are awake. Apparently they don't like to be outside until its bright daylight. *Do not be seen.* Set your Silent Speakers to channel three for the three of you, and report in with an update on channel two when you've finished, or by ten o'clock at the very latest. Are you clear?"

"Yes, sir!" said Ben, echoed quickly by the others.

Bourne and Jude melted away into the mist. They would search the dense, concealing vegetation where the Meddlers were more likely to be hidden, away from the people in the Commune. The three teenagers were left alone.

CHAPTER 5
BENJAMIN'S TUNNEL

Once Bourne and Jude had gone, Ben took charge. This was an adventure after his own heart. "Follow me," he said into the mouthpiece, and, in single file, they left the hideout.

Hugo was inclined to doubt Ben knew what he was doing as they crept through thick undergrowth and brambles, scratched, damp, and dirty, pushing through vegetation which all looked precisely the same. One thing that was reassuring was the high wall they glimpsed frequently close by; at least they were still walking along the boundary of the Commune.

Suddenly Ben stopped and inspected a tall tree. Hugo stepped closer, and Henrietta leaned over her brother's shoulder to peer at the small carving on the tree that Ben scrutinised.

"You see?" Ben's voice came into their earpieces. "You see? That's the mark Charlie and I made so we could find our way back to the secret tunnel!"

"C..A..B..S..T…" Henrietta spelt out slowly. "What on earth does it mean…?"

"Charlie and Ben's Secret Tunnel," said Hugo promptly. "I thought you had more imagination than that, Ben!"

"It's called exactly what it is," said Ben with dignity. "We might never have found it again if we had called it a silly name!" Secretly he wished they had used an elaborate code; it would have impressed the Wallop twins now. But at the time, he and Charlie, sleepy with the effect of the Sloths, had only been able to think of the most obvious 'code'. And of course his cousins didn't know about the effect of Sloths; they had been Christians and had worn the helmet of salvation far longer than he.

Hugo, eager to resume leadership of the little band, bent and examined the large opening which was concealed behind thick vegetation at the base of the tree. "You mean to say that…"

"It's the start of the tunnel," Ben said eagerly. "I can show you…"

But Hugo had already inserted his head and shoulders into the hole, and then his entire body vanished from view. Ben quickly followed.

"You go straight on," directed Ben.

"There's not exactly any other way to go, Ben," said Hugo drily.

Both boys had disappeared. Henrietta didn't waste any time. She took a deep breath – secretly she disliked small spaces – and courageously followed.

There was nothing unexpected or surprising about the tunnel under the wall. It appeared to have been there for many years. The earth floor was smooth, and large tree roots were comfortably entwined through the walls, looking as though they might well have made the strange tunnel themselves. There was one unpleasant moment on an otherwise unremarkable journey. They reached a junction where another tunnel snaked away in a different direction; the other tunnel was narrow and cramped and definitely more sinister than the one through which they crawled. At the junction a dead mole was directly in their way.

"Yuk!" said Henrietta.

They avoided it and crawled on – and reached the end of the tunnel. It was disappointingly un-dramatic. They simply came to a large opening in the roof above them. Like large rabbits at the entrance to their hole, they stood up: heads and shoulders exposed to dense, swirling mist.

It was immediately clear they had entered the grounds of Fearful Christian Commune. Dark, unfriendly stone walls belonging to a large mansion house rose through the mist and towered above them. Turrets and towers came and went from their view as the thick clouds swirled around them. There was an uncanny silence about the place; even the birds seemed loath to sing.

Henrietta shivered. "Why would anyone want to live here?"

It was far too eerie and quiet – and yet there was no feeling of peace.

"The people hide in their towers and imagine all kinds of weirdness and wickedness out here!" Ben said cheerfully. He, at least, was undismayed by the haunted greyness of the Commune. In fact, he was relishing how wonderful it felt to be here as a Christian dressed in his armour of God.[3] The folk who lived here didn't realise they had no need to hide away! They didn't know how great God is, and about the protection of the armour of God and so many other things! On previous visits Ben had been like them, and he and Charlie had imagined all kinds of ghosts and ghouls around them. But now Ben had protection about him which no ghostly presence could disturb.

Then, out of nowhere, they saw a *phantom* in the mist.

Henrietta clutched Hugo's arm. There really *was* a ghostly figure floating through the mist! Hugo pretended not to notice his sister's alarm. He was trying to act brave. Even Ben thought about ducking back into the tunnel and hiding away. But, not willing to show his fear and reluctance, and assuming the adventurous Wallop twins weren't afraid of anything, "We should follow it," he said, and boldly stepped from the hole.

Not for the world would Hugo admit his trepidation as he crept out of the safety of the hole after Ben and followed the unknown apparition further into the grounds of the Commune. Henrietta, certain she could do anything Hugo could, silently followed. Not one of them questioned why they should follow the unknown ghoul: they just did.

They were in an enclosed, decaying walled garden, following the grey apparition gliding through the fog – until it suddenly stopped. The *thing* stopped in the middle of a soggy square of badly trimmed grass. It looked like the spirit of an ancient prophet from a picture book of the Old Testament. Dressed in a ragged tunic, the creature raised thin, pale arms to the sky. Then one bare, bony leg was lifted high, and then slowly placed on the ground again, and then the other – the whole performance accompanied by curious grunts and groans as the stick-thin limbs moved in the most unnatural directions.

A very earthly giggle suddenly broke the trance of the three watchers. "Did you ever see anything like it?" exclaimed Ben. It had become apparent that the strange apparition was only a very elderly man doing exceedingly strange exercises. Ben strolled forward out of the thick mist towards him. It was unfortunate that the old man was in the middle of a delicate handstand: he gave a cry of alarm and fell flat on his back.

"Sorry about that," said Ben. "I only wanted to talk to you!"

The grey man stared wildly at the boy whose mouth was covered in a mask and whose voice he could not hear. He began to scuttle backwards over the damp grass, like a panicked crab.

"Don't go…" Ben began in his most friendly tone.

Henrietta's voice came into the earpiece. "Ben! He can't hear you!"

"I forgot!" Instantly Ben whipped his Silent Speaker mouthpiece away from his mouth and left it dangling oddly by his chin.

"Ben!" hissed Hugo. "That's against the rules! I don't think we're meant to take it off and talk to anyone…!"

But it was too late. "Can you hear me now?" Ben asked the old man kindly.

"W-w-what are you…?" stuttered the terrified elderly man.

"What are we doing here?" interpreted Ben, in his most soothing tone. "We're just passing through, you know, visiting, for research… to help, you see…"

"I don't think he *sees* at all," observed Hugo drily.

The old man was beyond astonished as two other figures peeled themselves from the mist and emerged to stand before him.

"H-h-how did you…?"

"Oh, never mind that," said Ben. "That's not important. What we need to know is if you've heard anything unusual, any voices, perhaps talking about Aletheia…? I mean, I know you always hear voices saying weird things, and probably they're not real voices at all, but what we really want to know is…"

"I think you're confusing him, Ben," said Henrietta. She, too, removed her mouthpiece. "We're Aletheians," she said. "We won't hurt you…"

"Henry!" hissed Hugo. "You've given us away! Now they'll know we entered the Commune grounds without permission, on a *secret mission*! That's against the rules too!"

"I think Jude said that one was an *unwritten* rule," said Ben. "I don't think it counts as much as a written one." He peered doubtfully at their new acquaintance. "Anyway, I don't think Mr… whoever he is, understands anything we've said so far. What…Is…Your…Name?" he asked slowly.

The old, grey man, now sat crossed-legged on the damp grass, was suddenly most indignant and apparently not stupid at all. "My name is nothing to do with *you*, you *wicked* children! You come here…

trespassing, intruding, thieving… *And* you've even disturbed the voices!"

Ben was now indignant too. "Hey! Steady on!" he said. "There's no need to be quite like that! We didn't mean to startle you, and you needn't think we don't like old people either! One of my best friends is an old man…"

Henrietta giggled wildly, quickly turning her laughter into a fit of coughing under the venomous glare of the old man.

"I wasn't trying to be funny, Henry!" Ben said sternly. "I was thinking of my friend, Dim View. Now he'll think I'm just being cheeky!"

"I don't think you're exactly helping, Ben!" said Hugo.

"You have no right to be here!" the old man said angrily, appearing more intelligent and cunning as the conversation proceeded. "You're interrupting my morning meditations and exercise! You've sent away the special voices! You've intruded on our peace and safety! They said no one ever came here! You are trespassing and must be held to account for…"

He was fumbling in his tatty tunic which concealed a surprisingly roomy pocket.

"Really!" retorted Ben. "There's no need to be so annoyed! We only wanted to talk to you…"

Suddenly a sharp, penetrating sound shattered the morning

stillness. The elderly man had removed a whistle from his pocket and sounded the alarm. "Now we'll see what happens to naughty children who trespass in our grounds!" he said.

The three adventurers were suddenly all action. The whistle had no sooner split the air with its piercing shriek, than they sped through the mist and back to the hole. They were none too soon either. Shadowy shapes emerged from the stone mansion and made their way to the walled garden. They could hear muffled voices through the thick, cloudy air.

Someone exclaimed, "Nil Vision sounded the alarm!"

"But he can't see a thing!" retorted another.

"Young people from Aletheia visiting the Commune?!" snapped a woman, her voice loud and shrill. "Have you gone mad, Nil? How could *children* possibly get into the grounds?! Now, get into the house before we're attacked by real enemies! Enough of your silly stories!"

"That's the woman in charge," said Ben. "She's called Mrs Dismay Defeatia. Charlie and I have spied on her before. She's pretty scary!"

"It's surprising any Meddlers would dare to be here with her in charge," remarked Hugo.

"Perhaps they aren't here," said Henrietta glumly. She and Ben had reattached their mouthpieces. She was beginning to realise that they might have messed up their mission and, in addition, landed their commanding officer in trouble with the Commune.

The angry, confused babble of voices began to fade away, heading back to the safety of the mansion.

"Perhaps it was Meddlers you saw, Nil…"

"It was a nasty boy! And another one! And a girl too! They looked like aliens…!"

"Nasty boy!" muttered Ben indignantly. "I thought I liked old people – until I met *him*!"

Mrs Defeatia's strident voice faded into the large grey mansion. "*Aliens*! I'll give you aliens if you even say one more word about this nonsense, Nil! We don't allow young people in here! We don't even like them! We're hiding from real dangers, and now we've probably let every enemy within ten miles know where we are…!"

CHAPTER 6
HENRIETTA ON HER OWN

"All OK?" A cheerful voice echoed suddenly in their earpieces.

"Dusty!" exclaimed Hugo. "I forgot you were listening in!" In the excitement of the incident with Nil Vision they had almost forgotten they were supposed to be tracking Meddlers.

"Not listening in, exactly, but we're tracking your movements. You moved pretty quickly a moment ago; I wondered if you'd found the Meddlers and they were chasing you!"

"Uh, not exactly." Hugo hoped he wouldn't have to explain about Nil Vision; Mr Vision didn't really make a lot of sense.

"Anyway, we've got some interesting signals coming from your current location," explained Dusty.

The three teenagers scanned the grubby hole in the ground in which they crouched. It seemed incredibly unlikely that there was any *interesting signal* here, but they knew better than to doubt Dusty.

"There's a high concentration of white vapour south-south-east of your current location. You're showing very close to it; it's only about twenty metres from you."

"Make sure you have the Spy Nozzle ready…" Flair's voice sounded clearly in their earpieces.

Of course they would. Despite the incident with Nil Vision, they did know some of the procedures they should follow. But Flair just *had* to say it anyway.

They began crawling back through the dirty tunnel, following the light shining from their Bibles which were safety attached to their belts, always at their side. They crawled in silence. Thin tendrils of grubby white mist began to curl about them even here. Henrietta was thinking how glad she would be to get out of the tunnel into the fresh air again when she stopped abruptly in surprise. They had reached the small junction where the dirtier, narrower, less enticing tunnel snaked away into the unknown.

"Hugo!"

"We'll be out of here soon, Henry," panted Hugo. "Keep going…"

"Stop!" hissed Henrietta. "It's gone! Hugo, stop!"

Hugo paused, trying to see back over his shoulder, past Ben, to Henrietta. "What's gone?"

"The dead mole!"

Ben managed to shift around. He examined the junction where the dead mole had most certainly been a short while earlier. "She's right!" he confirmed. "It's definitely gone!"

"*Something* must have been here!" exclaimed Henrietta.

Ben grinned. "Nil Vision looked hungry enough to eat a mole!"

Hugo didn't laugh. Slowly he asked, "Do *Meddlers* eat moles?"

"Seems like just the type of nasty, disgusting thing they *might* do!" Ben seldom needed actual evidence to believe an interesting theory.

"White mist!" exclaimed Henrietta. "Hugo, there are bits of white mist coming from that narrow tunnel!"

Hugo was thinking hard. The narrow tunnel! Was it possible the Meddlers were meeting underground? It might fit with Dusty's directions… But neither he nor Ben could possibly fit in that enclosed space. It was built for far smaller creatures than growing boys. His sister, Henry, however, was smaller and slighter than the boys. "Henry…"

"I know what you're going to say, Hugo," Henrietta's voice trembled.

"Do you? Can't say I know what he's talking about!" said Ben.

"I'll go," said Henrietta. "Pass the Spy Nozzle and let me go quick, before I change my mind!"

Suddenly the exciting adventure into Err on a secret mission had taken a sinister turn. It was all very well exploring the unknown with Hugo and Ben, with the reassuring presence of Bourne Faithful who could surely tackle any enemy; it was all very well feeling part of an important team who might discover amazing things for the good of Aletheia. Adventures were great when they were going well.

But now, unexpectedly, Henrietta was on her own. She crawled cautiously through the dark, dirty, far-too-narrow tunnel. She was linked with Hugo and Ben through the Silent Speakers, but the boys could no longer help her.

Hugo's voice was continually encouraging her through her earpiece. "Alright, Henry? Anything to report?"

"Mist! Only mist!" said Henrietta grimly.

There was no need for further directions; the mist was growing thicker, shifting down the tunnel and twisting around her like a chilling, evil spell. It was clammy and cold in a way that the outdoor mist had not been. It was coming from somewhere or something that was plain *evil*. That much she *just knew*, even if she could never hope to explain it to the others. She kept her eyes fixed on the light of the Bible which still clung to her side, warm and strong and the only light that could penetrate this dark, unfriendly place. She wished she could hold it in her hands and open its pages. It would flood the place with brightness which would dispel these eerie grey-white shifting shadows. But she needed both her hands to feel her way forward; she tried not to think how she would get back.

Dusty's voice from the Control Room came through her earpiece. He sounded so reassuringly cheerful and encouraging. "According to our coordinates, we can see you're nearly there, Henry!"

"There's so much mist," panted Henrietta as she squeezed through another horribly tight turn in the twisting tunnel. She breathed in to get through the space in the earth-covered rocks. There would definitely be no running away from the Meddlers ahead – assuming they were there. "This mist is different to the other mist, it's…"

"Yes?" prompted Dusty.

"It's…it makes you feel cold and numb…"

"What else about the mist?" urged Flair, who was thinking of collecting information for scientific analysis.

"It smells like something rotten… like… like I would imagine *death* to smell. It's almost… almost as if it's solid, not mist at all… like liquid poison… and it's not so much white as dirty grey…"

"Remember, nothing can harm you in your armour of God!" came her brother's voice.

Ben added his own style of encouragement. "You're almost as cool as a boy!"

"That's all I need!" Henrietta managed to retort. She fixed her eyes on the light of her Bible again. The mist was even worse now. She had a feeling that around this next corner…

"I'm getting noise feed on the Spy Nozzle!" Dusty's voice, clearly excited. "You've found them, Henry! I do believe it might be the Meddlers…!"

Flair's clipped instructions came next. "If you could just get a little closer, and remember to extend the Spy Nozzle…"

"*You* jolly well come here and extend the Spy Nozzle!" muttered Henrietta.

Ben sniggered.

"Henry?"

"Nothing," Henrietta said more distinctly. After all, it wasn't Flair's fault that she was trapped in a creepy, increasingly terrifying tunnel; Flair couldn't see how awful it was here.

Henrietta unstrapped the slender, metal rod from her wrist. It pulled apart from within itself, extending like fine wire, to whatever length you wanted it. Cautiously she held the Spy Nozzle in front of her. Slowly she turned the corner.

CHAPTER 7
MEDDLERS!

White cloud concealed the meeting which was taking place only metres away from Henrietta in an earthen cave under the grounds of the Fearful Christian Commune. She could see no detail of the Meddlers in their grey-white, misty jackets. The vapour, or smoke, or whatever it was, came from them and obscured their small, gangling outlines. They looked like horrible, skeletal, miniature ghosts. But there was no doubt that they were real. Strange mutterings – some of them in rhyme – punctured the thick air around her. A Meddler leader led the discord. Like a ghastly conductor he helped his minions to learn the lies that they would use to destroy the city of Truth: for the Meddlers were meeting to discuss their schemes for the downfall of Aletheia.

"Zee Chief iz a cheatz who will zoon know defeatz…" There was a peculiar foreign accent, a fuzzy sounding zzz which slurred everything they said. But, despite that, the White-Jacket Meddlers, being one of the more intelligent types of Meddler, spoke with surprising clarity.

Of course, it wasn't hard to understand this particular portion of rhyme. It was immediately apparent that at least part of the Meddlers' plan was, indeed, to ruin the character of the chief people of Aletheia

– and this silly line was about making the Chief appear to be a cheat. Would they plant evidence that Chief Steadfast was corrupt? Would they make it appear as if he took bribes?

Henrietta was sincerely glad she did not have to remember the secrets spoken at this terrible gathering. In her ear, the reassuring tones of Dusty told her she was quite close enough to capture the information, firmly overriding Flair's desire for "just a bit closer…" She pressed herself into a crevice which proved a convenient hiding place. The mist was suffocating. Each breath was like a breath of poison – thick and heavy and laced with dead and decaying things.

"Zee Mazterz at zchool will zoon be zee foolz…"

Henrietta grimaced. So, they would attack her formidable Headmaster, the honourable Mr Mustardpot, too, would they? Having a healthy respect for her Headmaster, she wondered who would come off the best in that particular encounter…

"Zee Doctorz iz badz and mozt zertainly madz…"

Well, there were plenty of people in Aletheia who considered the brilliant Dr Pentone somewhat *mad*, but they loved and respected him all the same. What evidence would the Meddlers concoct to show that the good doctor was bad?

"Zee Judge is unfair, of her judgementz bewarez…"

So, Chief Judge, Sagacia Steady, would not be spared. There was plenty about the judgement of Aletheia the land of Err did not like: it definitely did not conform to their ideas that there was no right or wrong and that everything was a matter of choice and opinion. No, it would not take much for the Council of Err to make a case against Chief Judge Steady.

The chanting of the weird and silly rhymes and other chatter continued. Even more worrying than attacking the characters of the leaders of Aletheia, the Meddlers also spoke about their plans to undermine the Truth of the Bible too. Now, what the listening Aletheians *really* needed to know was where the Meddlers' headquarters – the Rumour Mill – was located. Attacking the Rumour Mill was Aletheia's best hope of destroying the source of the poisonous lies. If they could destroy the Rumour Mill, it would clear away, if only for a time, the muddle and lies of the Meddlers and allow people to respond to Bible Truth.

An authoritative Meddler voice, with only the slightest accent, now spoke. "Fellowz, we be on zee brink of our greatezt meddle yet!"

Henrietta could hear Dusty's quick intake of breath. She knew he was recording every word. The others were silently waiting...

There was a chorus of Meddler cheers from the chamber, and thick, dirty-grey vapour spewed thickly around Henrietta. The rancid air made her feel sick. This was the taste of lies and slander. The Spy

Nozzle in her hand trembled.

"Keep the Spy Nozzle steady," Flair instructed.

Henrietta bit her lip. She would like to tell Flair what she could do with the Spy Nozzle...

"Our great home, our Rumour Millz..." the Meddler leader was continuing to speak, "...is zee zentre of our planz..."

Suddenly, abruptly, the leader stopped.

"Henry?" Flair's voice again, sounding frantic now. "You didn't drop the Spy Nozzle, did you? This bit is important!"

"No, I jolly well didn't drop the Nozzle!" Henrietta hissed into the Silent Speaker. Around her thick grey vapour churned in disgusting clouds. It was increasing in quantity and density. The rumbles of what she imagined was consternation echoed around the earth-cave within a hand's reach of her. She didn't like to think what she would do if the Meddlers emptied en masse and flocked around her; she still didn't know how she would ever get out of this impossibly tight tunnel. "Something's up," she muttered.

"Stay put for a moment longer," encouraged Dusty.

"It iz spiez..." a Meddler voice with a heavier Meddle-accent was explaining. "Wez arez overheard by ze humanz!"

"Have they seen you, Henry?" Flair sounded urgent and disappointed.

Henrietta was puzzled. "I don't see how they could!"

"We haz no fear of humanz!" came the clearer, decisive voice of the Meddler leader. "But we continue in anozer placez."

"Humanz too meddled to rememberz…" another Meddler said scornfully. For a moment they wondered if they might learn the secret location of the Rumour Mill after all. If the Meddlers thought that whoever was present would be too befuddled to remember, they might remain. But,

"Humanz might have inventionz," said the leader wisely. "We go."

And go they did.

There was no frantic rush of Meddlers from their underground meeting place. Henrietta was not beset with flocking Meddlers. There was no panic. If they thought they had been overheard, they weren't concerned. Gradually the babble of Meddlers grew distant and faded away in another direction entirely, until there was nothing at all. Only silence. The churning, dirty vapour slowly thinned until Henrietta could see again.

"Better make your way back, Henry." Hugo sounded disappointed. They all were. They seemed so close to vital information. What could have happened to alert the Meddlers to Henry's presence?

Henrietta knew they all suspected she had done something wrong. She viewed the way she had come and shuddered. Could she fit through the tunnel once more and retrace her steps?

"I'm going to check where the Meddlers were meeting. They seemed to leave another way…" She moved from her hiding place and rounded the final corner.

She stopped in astonishment.

Crouching behind a rock, brushing dirt from his very grubby clothes, was a classmate from school.

It was Charlie Steady.

Charlie was no less surprised to see Henrietta than she was to see him.

"What on earth are you doing here?!" exclaimed Henrietta.

Charlie stared at her blankly. He looked very sick, which didn't surprise Henrietta in the least. He had been breathing in the disgusting vapour too, and Charlie didn't have the protection of the armour of God.[3] She didn't like to imagine what the Meddlers' poisonous air might do to someone who was unprotected.

There was a babble of voices in her earpiece. "What is it…?!"

"It's Charlie Steady!" exclaimed Henrietta. Then she remembered that Charlie, who was still staring at her blankly, couldn't hear anything she was saying through the Silent Speaker. She removed her mouthpiece. It no longer seemed important to keep quiet – not now that Charlie had interrupted their most important mission: for it was clear *Charlie* was the human presence which had stopped the flow of information.

"Enryz?" Charlie was peering at her peculiarly. Evidently he wasn't sure what was happening.

"Of course I'm Henry! Are you alright, Charlie? You sound weird! You do realise that you've just interrupted a most important mission?!"

"No, of courz I don't realisez!" retorted Charlie. "Howz could Iz when nobody tellz mez? Zat'z why I followed you all zecretly! I knew Benz waz up to somethinz wiz you all… buz I lostz you in zee tunnelz! But zere'z anozer way in andz out, you zee, one I juz dizcovered todayz when I waz trying to followz you all and not be zeen. Juzt to zee what youz all up to, you know, becauz no one tellz me anything…!"

Henrietta heaved a deep sigh. She liked Charlie Steady, and his mischief definitely kept them amused at school. But Charlie was *the most* exasperating person to argue with, especially with this weird accent which made him sound *just like one of the Meddlers*! The main thing was to get out of there, and then they could figure out what on earth had happened to Charlie.

"Never mind all that now," she said. "If you happen to know something useful – like a different way out of here other than the horrible tunnel I came down – you can at least show me the way!"

Through the distinctly grey pallor of his usually healthy face, Charlie looked slightly cheered. He excelled in finding a way out of tricky situations. It hadn't been any fun being on his own all day, and for the last hour he had been stuck in this labyrinth of underground tunnels, swallowing foul-tasting, dirty-looking vapour from a bunch of grubby-white Meddlers. There was even one rather disgustingly munching on a dead mole!

"Zere'z definitely anozer wayz." Charlie took charge of the situation, glad to play the leader. "We'z go zee wayz zee Meddlerz went!" Charlie continued. "I zaw zem! Come on! Ziz wayz…!"

They crossed the low chamber. Henrietta fervently hoped that this new route would be larger than just Meddler size. They began to crawl down another narrow tunnel. It appeared, after all, to be made by something larger than a Meddler; it was just big enough for them. Charlie led the way, clutching a small torch which cast feeble light and made gloomy shadows. Henrietta relied on the light of her Bible.[4] It was powerful and alive and the light chased all the shadows away.

Suddenly Charlie stopped. "We'z come to zee end!"

Ahead of them was a dirt wall; the sides of the tunnel were earth and rock and unyielding. As Charlie examined the ceiling in the light of his feeble torch, Henrietta scrutinised Charlie in the light of her Bible. It seemed to her that, as well as his strange accent, his hair and skin were decidedly odd: dirty-grey… a bit like… a bit like the colour of the Meddlers' vapour. She decided that now was not the time to investigate. They needed to get out of this underground place. Then they could figure out exactly what had happened to Charlie.

"I zink wez go up!" said Charlie.

A tiny mechanism, small enough for a Meddler to manage, yielded easily when Charlie pressed it. A neat square cover of dirt lifted upwards, and Charlie squeezed his head, then his shoulders, through the small space. Soil and a couple of worms settled on his strange grey hair.

"We'z got out alright! Come on, Henryz! Zere'z a weird manz here, but other zan zat, I zink we'z alright!"

He scrambled through the hole and vanished from sight.

Cautiously, Henrietta put her head through the hole in the ground. Slowly, she looked around.

Henrietta had seen this forlorn patch of garden before. They were once more in the grounds of the Fearful Christian Commune. In fact, they had appeared through the earth in the middle of the square of grass she had already visited that same strange day. And on that same patch of grass… was the same ragged old man, Mr Nil Vision!

Henrietta scrambled free and Charlie fitted the small square of turf back onto the now enlarged hole. The hole was only intended to be the size of a few Meddlers, but now it was roughly enlarged to the size of a boy and girl. The square of earth sagged down on one side and didn't seem to fit back properly at all.

Charlie shrugged carelessly. "Never mindz. But you might fallz through zee groundz, zir! I don't zink you should goz near it!"

His remark was addressed to the thin, ragged old man who had not long resumed his morning 'meditations' and was now once more sprawled on the ground, regarding them with the utmost horror.

Tremulously, he kept repeating, "They'll never believe me. They'll never believe me! *She'll* never believe me!"

"She probably won't, Mr Vision. Better not say anything about it," suggested Henrietta.

Charlie stared at the strange old man with interest. "Do youz already know ziz old chapz?"

"We've already bumped into him once today!"

"The voices from the earth!" mumbled Nil Vision. "I was hearing voices from the *Square of Doom* where I do my exercises! It's special here...!"

"Not zo zpecial now, I'z afraid," remarked Charlie. "Honeztly, you'll fallz through zee earth into zee tunnelz if you do yourz exercizez here!"

Henrietta tried to explain. "They were Meddlers speaking. *They* were the voices you heard. I expect you heard them when they left just now. They came through the same way we just did, didn't they?"

"Earth-voices speaking to me… Messages… Doom, they speak of doom…"

"Theyz would do, zee nazty blighterz!" agreed Charlie.

The old man studied Charlie. "Are you-are you one of th-them…?" he stuttered tremblingly.

"No, I'z not!" exclaimed Charlie indignantly. "Completely battyz," he added in an aside to Henrietta. "Whyz on earthz would he zink zat?!"

Henrietta didn't know what to say. How could she explain that it was because Charlie sounded, and indeed, looked, like a White-Jacket Meddler? "Um, sorry to disturb you again, Mr Vision." She tugged on Charlie's arm. "If you ever feel like getting away from Mrs Defeatia, you're always welcome in Aletheia!"

They left Nil Vision on the *Square of Doom*. Henrietta hurried Charlie away. Something was seriously wrong with him. It was time to get him back to the safety of Aletheia.

CHAPTER 8
DR PENTONE AT WORK

On their return from Fearful Christian Commune, Bourne and Jude lost no time in contacting Dr Theo Pentone. Charlie's grey face and hair and strange accent were obvious to all of them except Charlie himself. It appeared he had imbibed, and was now infected by, White-Jacket Meddler poison, and if anyone would know what to do about the effects of the poison, it was the clever doctor.

It was a mark of the strangeness and significance of events that Dr Pentone immediately rushed across to the Judges' Academy to join them. Without preamble or pleasantries, he went straight to Charlie who stayed seated on a chair in Jude's office. He peered closely at him, clearly very intrigued.

Rather belligerently, Charlie stared back. "What'ze looking atz?" he asked. Whatever else the Meddlers had done to Charlie, they had also affected his usual amiability.

"His accent, yes, I see what you mean…" Dr Pentone wasn't at all put off by difficult patients. He removed a magnifying glass from his lab coat pocket and scrutinised Charlie's skin and hair, ignoring Charlie's loud, annoyed "Oy!"

"Of course, the poisonous vapour could never stick to the armour of

God," remarked the doctor, as if he was talking to himself. "Nothing of Err can penetrate that covering! But the fact that someone was there without any protection… what an extraordinary turn of events!"

"I was wondering whether this unusual situation could work to our advantage," said Jude.

Dr Pentone smiled grimly. "I was just wondering the same thing myself!"

"You mean we could analyse the poison…" Bourne looked between his brother and Theo Pentone.

The doctor nodded. "Exactly. We have the most unexpected sample of Meddler poison in this young man. It's possible that this might even help us to trace the Meddlers…"

Charlie appeared mostly oblivious of this discussion. On the whole he was pleased to be part of this meeting and so-called *Team Meddler*. He was once more with his friend Ben, and, aside from a scuffle when he had teased Ben about his *girlfriend* Flair, to which Ben reacted with surprising violence, all seemed *almost* well.

"Could a sample of the poison be extracted from ordinary objects, such as clothes, or the torch that Charlie carried?" asked Jude.

"I think it would be best to take a sample of his hair – which appears to have thoroughly imbibed the poison, right into the very roots…"

"His hair even *smells* like the horrible decay of the Meddlers' lies!"

mumbled Henrietta. As frustrating as it was that Charlie had ruined their mission, it was impossible not to feel pity for his poor, grey, confused state now.

Once more, Dr Pentone smiled grimly. "I've smelt worse," he said.

The others didn't even want to imagine *what*.

"Ben, fetch the scissors from Jude's desk," said Bourne.

Ben placed the scissors in Dr Pentone's outstretched hand. The doctor snipped a random chunk of fair-cum-grey hair from Charlie's head. Theo Pentone was no barber; there was now a noticeable ragged gap on Charlie's head. The doctor placed the hair in one of the see-through bags he also carried in his pocket. "I'll get it analysed as soon as possible," he said. "In the meantime, I suggest you carry on with your other investigations. They might still be needed."

"Dusty, Flair – do what you can to further analyse white mist weather patterns and narrow down possible locations of the Meddlers," instructed Jude. "Although it's doubtful that this method will be precise enough to take us to the Rumour Mill," he added.

"But it's worth a try," agreed Bourne. "We also now know more about the poison of the White-Jackets – which isn't natural cloud, and which probably accounts for Charlie not being able to remember anything."

Charlie kept silent. Bourne Faithful didn't miss a trick! Charlie had wanted to contribute to the discussion, but, although he had tried not to let the others know, the dense, sickening vapour hadn't let him think at all. It was the one reason that the Meddlers hadn't searched for or attacked him. The clever White-Jacket Meddlers knew the effect their poison had; they knew that normally their discussion could not be remembered by anyone. Of course, they didn't know about the protection of the armour of God and the helmet of salvation,[3] or about the clever listening devices invented by the Academy of Soldiers-of-the-Cross. But they suspected enough to move on.

Dr Pentone once more bent down and searched Charlie's face. He looked at him kindly, even compassionately. "I want you to listen very carefully, son," he said.

"I alwayz listenz carefully!"

Dr Pentone explained, "You have been polluted by the Meddlers' poison. You have imbibed some of their character too. We will try to treat you, but there's only one way to be absolutely free from the poison of lies and slander which now infect you…"

Charlie shrugged. He felt fine; he didn't know why the others stared at him so strangely. Why were they all looking at him as if he had two heads? As for the rest, the lecture this odd, disconcerting doctor gave about only the cleansing offered by God, through the sacrifice of the Lord Jesus, being able to cleanse him[5]…

He had heard it all before.

Dr Theo Pentone's favourite moments were undoubtedly the ones he spent in his Experimentation Laboratory. This was his own domain. It was situated within the vast Academy of Soldiers-of-the-Cross, on one of the lower floors – beneath ground level, with tiny windows high up, peeping at the feet of the people who walked by.

It was a very tall room, and the immense stone walls were lined with shelves upon shelves containing his treasures: ancient, sometimes stained and torn books; wooden models of strange creatures and body parts; specimens – fascinating and sometimes gruesome – in glass jars; intriguing locked boxes; shiny, sharp, complex pieces of scientific equipment (some of his own invention); rows upon rows of samples in test tubes and jars – all precisely labelled and filed exactly where they should be.

Unusually, today Dr Pentone had an assistant: a tall, gangly lad wearing thick-rimmed glasses and an amiable, earnest expression. Dusty Addle had entered the doctor's laboratory.

Laid out on the long white table was an assortment of samples he had taken from his shelves. In one glass jar, incongruously labelled 'Strawberry Jam', there was a disgusting creature preserved in unknown liquid. This was a Fretter leader – once an important part of a plot to destroy the food sources of the city of Aletheia.[6] The creature had exploded as part of Dr Pentone's efforts to neutralise its evil; now it floated in preserving liquid, its burnt, grotesque body stuck in time… and, oddly, once more it had its uses.

Close by the 'Strawberry Jam' jar, there was a glass vial containing sick-green goo; a jar containing an apple and a pear, preserved in vomit-green coloured liquid; a white sheet of paper upon which was laid the sample of Charlie's grey-coated hair; a large glass vial, supported by a metal stand and situated above a small fire; and various other pieces of scientific equipment.

"Just a drop or two of the liquid that rascal is floating in," directed the doctor to Dusty, indicating the Fretter leader, now preserved in smouldering and disgusting decay. He handed Dusty a small syringe.

Dusty tried to ignore the stench of rotten eggs when he removed the lid. He carefully extracted a couple of drops of the liquid from the top of the jar.

"He always was a rancid chap! Poisonous through and through!" remarked Dr Pentone.

Dusty dropped the liquid he had collected into the large glass vial which was beginning to bubble above the small fire. There was a WHOOSH of smoke which surprised him and once more filled the air with the horrible smell of extremely rotten eggs.

Dr Pentone watched the bubbling liquid with avid interest. The gurgling, steaming liquid turned bright green, before gradually mixing with the silvery-grey liquid in the pot, until it all became a wonderful shiny grey.

"As I suspected," the doctor said. "The root of the two poisons, the Fretter poison from the Meddlers of Blight, and the poison from the White-Jacket Meddlers, is the same – although they have vastly different effects on people." He hummed an off-key hymn-tune as he took a sample of the seething liquid. "Evil always ultimately stems from the same source," he said. "But we are all susceptible in different ways…" He squirted the sample of liquid he had taken into a small glass vial, and then labelled it in his own unique squiggly writing: '*Basic Formula of Meddler Poison, 19 April*'.

As the sample of gleaming grey liquid – like silvery mercury – continued to bubble, the doctor began to extract minute samples of the once fair, now grey-coated, hair. With Dusty's assistance, they worked for hours – through lunchtime and on towards teatime – producing a sample of grey powder from the hair. Now they could compare the Meddlers' poison from Charlie's hair with the still gurgling Meddler poison formula. Dr Pentone didn't care about missing meals; Dusty tried to cover up the noise of his rumbling stomach, but he didn't think the doctor would have noticed anyway.

At teatime, a neat old lady, wearing a spotless white apron, entered the doctor's laboratory without permission, bearing a tray of sandwiches and cakes. She put it on a corner of the table, wrinkling her nose at the still lingering smell of rotten eggs. "I suppose you've missed lunch, Theo?" she said sternly.

"Leave the tray there," said the doctor absentmindedly. Then he remembered Dusty. "I don't suppose you've met my mother?"

Dusty gaped and the old lady smiled. "Whatever have you been up to all these hours?" she asked. She scanned with interest the earnest boy who mumbled a polite greeting. She knew he must have special talent for Theo to allow him to assist in this way.

"We have today discovered the basic formula for Meddler poison. Which means…"

"It means you can more easily identify and detect the poison in other samples, I suppose," said his mother. "Is this to do with the poisoning of the Steady boy?"

"Exactly!" agreed the doctor. "Mother is far cleverer than I am," he added drily. "She wouldn't have had to miss lunch to get as far as we have today!"

The old lady laughed. "Away with you!" she said. "I don't have time to hang around and watch your bumbling experiments!" But all the same, her bright eyes were flitting about the room; this was, indeed, exactly what she would like to do.

When she had gone, Dusty tucked into the delicious sandwiches and cream cakes, and poured two cups of tea from the dainty teapot. Dr Pentone ignored the food, and his own cup of tea: he was very near the end of his experiment, about to discover…

"Here…" He handed Dusty a mask. "If this is what I suspect it to be, even this small amount could affect our minds…" He quickly fitted his own mask.

Dusty hastily swallowed yet another dainty cake.

Dr Pentone placed the small sample of grey they had extracted from the once-fair hair into a large glass tube which already contained a sample of the strangely beautiful bubbling liquid. Immediately there was a puff of grey-white smoke, and the liquid began to spew clouds of vapour. Dr Pentone hastily slapped a lid on the top of the test tube and removed his mask. He regarded Dusty soberly. "Alright?" he asked.

"Ztrange…I mean…" Dusty swallowed. If the truth were told, he felt very odd, and what an awful smell had emanated from that smoke! It was even worse than the rotten eggs of the green blight poison! "I mean, that felt *strange*," he said, making an effort to pronounce the *s*. Speaking with a *z* felt horribly like listening to one of those Meddlers they had recorded…

Dr Pentone was examining him strangely. "Sorry, son," he said, "I should have waited until I was sure you were wearing your mask, but I was never that great at health and safety! No permanent harm done, I assure you you'll be fine shortly!"

"But did we do it?" asked Dusty as his head cleared. "Is that *smoke…?*"

Dr Pentone nodded. From being exuberant and excited with his peculiar experiments, he was now sober. "We did it," he said. "I believe we have created a sample of the White-Jacket Meddler poison, and that means…"

"It means that Charlie Steady is definitely infected by it, doesn't it?"

Once more, Dr Pentone nodded.

"And can we work on a cure, sir?" asked Dusty eagerly.

Dr Pentone shook his head. "There is no need to work on any cure."

"But…"

"We can only treat the symptoms Charlie has. There is already a complete cure available, but Charlie must choose to receive it. It is the salvation which is found in the person of the Lord Jesus."[2]

CHAPTER 9
THE PRAYER ACADEMY

To the members of *Team Meddler*, time was of the essence. The White-Jacket Meddlers had confirmed that the respected leaders of Aletheia would be targeted and slandered by them, and Bible Truth, too, would be attacked. Surely not a moment should be lost in discovering and destroying these small, pesky mechanised creatures of Err, and their home – the Rumour Mill. It was therefore surprising and unwelcome that preparations seemed slow and cautious.

"Why, sir?" Henrietta enquired of her commanding officer, Bourne Faithful, as she carried out her duties as his assistant-cum-gofer the following week. "Why don't we set off at once and destroy them?"

Bourne was busy analysing a report that Henrietta had just brought to him from Dusty. It was the report of Dr Pentone's experiments with the Meddler poison. "We have to discover their location first," he remarked.

"Well, bomb everywhere that there is mist or cloud then!" sighed Henrietta, exasperated by the inaction.

Bourne scribbled on the corner of the report and handed it back to Henrietta. "Straight back to Dusty," he directed. "He'll take it to Dr Pentone."

Henrietta sighed again and prepared to speed back through the corridors of the Academy to the Central Control Room once more. Why all the analyses and research and reports and delays? She wished they would all hurry up and get on with the action.

"Why all the haste, anyway?" asked Bourne.

Henrietta detected the twinkle in his eye. She knew her cousin was as anxious for action as she was. "Shouldn't we be stopping the lies before they can do any damage to the leaders? It's not fair on them, and people might believe them…"

"People will always believe lies if they prefer them to the Truth," observed Bourne. "But this isn't only about the leaders and their reputations. We fight to defend and uphold the Truth! If we destroy the hotbed of Meddlers which is the Rumour Mill, we will destroy a lot of the lies and muddle of the Meddlers – at least for a time. Then others in the land of Err might come to know the Truth."

"But that still makes it important to get on with it, doesn't it?"

Bourne asked, "Just out of interest, Henry, how do you propose we destroy the Rumour Mill? Supposing we find it – as easily as you appear to anticipate – how do we then overcome it and destroy its evil?"

"With the Water of Sound Doctrine?" Henrietta asked hopefully. During the war, she had seen the power of the water which represented the whole Truth of the Word of God. It was a remarkable weapon![1] Surely it could simply wash away the lies of the Meddlers too, and wash this awful Rumour Mill – whatever it was – down the drain, to the sewers where it belonged!

"The Water of Sound Doctrine is a great weapon against the *error* of our enemies," Bourne agreed. "But there is something else we need to prepare to overcome the poisonous slander and lies we expect to encounter."

"What is it?" asked Henrietta eagerly. "Where is it being prepared?"

"I think, perhaps, you and your colleagues had better pay a visit to the Prayer Academy and find out," said Bourne. "Since it is just possible you may be called on to play a further part in locating the Rumour Mill, you ought to know what's going on behind the scenes. You must visit Supplication…"

Henrietta was suddenly ready to dance from the room. She was desperate to confer with the others, desperate for some action.

"Henry…?"

Henrietta paused at the door one final time. "Yes, sir?"

"You *are* paying attention at school, aren't you?"

"Um…" For the moment Henrietta was bemused. She definitely failed to see the connection between school and this conversation. "Yes, sir, of course, sir…!"

Bourne shook his head as his young assistant sped away. The kids might yet be called upon to play a part in locating the Rumour Mill. Were they aware of the importance of their school theme – a subject as seemingly simple and innocuous as *love*?

"I still don't understand *why* Bourne thinks it would be a good idea to visit the Prayer Academy!" remarked Hugo. "I wish you had asked more questions about it, Henry; it might be important!"

"I don't care why we're going," admitted Ben. "I've never been to the Prayer Academy before and I've always wondered what it was like."

Henrietta craned her neck to gaze upwards, a *long way* upwards, to the tall towers of the Prayer Academy. It was the highest building in Aletheia. It towered over everything else around – over everything, that is, apart from the cross. "You don't know what it's like working for Bourne," she said mildly to her brother's criticism. "You don't dare ask too many questions!"

Josie Faithful, who was the last of the four students making their way to the Prayer Academy, was rummaging in her neat and tidy bag. "When I got the message to join you, I read about the Prayer Academy's *Supplication Room* in the library at the Judges' Academy."

Ben stared at her. Organisation always surprised him, and distant-cousin Josie Faithful was the most organised person he knew. She wasn't as serious and studious as Flair, of course – but then, she wasn't as weird or gullible either. Whenever time allowed away from school, she worked with *The Truth*, the official newspaper of Aletheia. She was always researching something and writing about it. In the war she even helped write a column for the newspaper.[1]

"I didn't know they had books about the Prayer Academy," said Ben, thinking it a safe response, but Josie merely looked amazed at his ignorance.

"Well, anyway, they do," she said briskly.

"What do they say about it, Jo?" prompted Hugo. "What do they *do* in this room called *Supplication?*"

"It's to do with united prayer," explained Josie. "Groups of people meet together to focus on a specific problem or need, and they create… well, they create a token – you know, as a pledge that they'll be praying – and this can then be used on the problem, you see?" Josie was skim-reading, and walking, and talking at the same time.

"Like Mrs De Voté's knitted square!" exclaimed Henrietta.

Ben was curious. "Really?"

"We used it in the purple storm,"[7] said Henrietta. "You must have heard of *that*, Ben!"

Ben nodded. *Everyone* had heard of the biggest storm in the land of

Err in recent times. In his opinion, his cousins had been lucky to land in the middle of it!

They reached the imposing front of the towering Prayer Academy. Hugo entered the massive open doorway more confidently than he felt. They had been welcome here in the past, but would they be allowed the free access they needed this time? Parts of the Prayer Academy were protected. There were things here that were guarded and secret; unchartered nooks and crannies which very few had ever discovered. There was about the whole place an aura of unfathomable tranquillity: silence which echoed with unheard whispers, almost like prayer itself. The uninitiated couldn't just wander around wherever they wanted, disturbing the work of prayer.

The front door guard, wearing the pristine white and gold uniform of the Academy, looked up with a pleased expression when he observed the four students. Immediately, he looked between Henrietta and Josie. "Miss Wallop?"

Henrietta was amazed.

"That's me!"

"Lieutenant Faithful sent a message to expect you and some companions," said the guard. "You're here to visit Supplication? It's currently under guard, you see, so you'll need special passes..." He bent and rummaged in his desk drawer, sheepishly removing his lunchtime sandwiches. Underneath the sandwiches was a neat envelope, and in the envelope were four slender golden cards. "Special passes have been prepared for you, just as the Lieutenant requested."

Henrietta was delighted when the guard handed her the four golden cards. For once, it felt as if she was in charge instead of Hugo. Solemnly, she passed the cards around to the others. Their names were inscribed on them, along with a different verse from the Bible about prayer. *Praying always with all prayer and supplication in the Spirit, being watchful to this end with all perseverance and supplication for all the saints.*[8] Henrietta read the delicately inscribed words on her golden card.

Josie examined her beautiful card. *Be anxious for nothing, but in everything by prayer and supplication, with thanksgiving, let your requests be made known to God; and the peace of God, which surpasses all understanding, will guard your hearts and minds through Christ Jesus.*[9] With the utmost care she placed it in a safe pocket and zipped it up. "The last time we were here we were given a golden pin, remember?"

she said.

Hugo nodded. "Yes, and we had to give them back at the end," he said regretfully, admiring his golden card. He would never want to return it.

"Pins are a lower level of access," remarked the guard. "For access to Supplication you need cards. It's particularly important just now, you see? And you get to keep the cards. They're made specifically to meet *your* needs; they're no good to anyone else."

They hurried to the large, round, hollow pillar in the centre of the hall – inside which was the super-fast elevator which took you wherever you needed to go within the Prayer Academy. Hugo and Henrietta and Josie had been here before. To Ben, everything was new. And, since he seldom pretended to be what he was not, he gawked at everything around him and didn't bother pretending he was a seasoned pro at the Prayer Academy – the way the others might have preferred.

A girl was polishing the outside of the elevator, humming happily as she worked.

"Crystal!" exclaimed Henrietta. She had first met Crystal during the war, when Crystal had become a Christian.[1] Crystal smiled radiantly at the newcomers. She had moved to Aletheia after the war, and, since she had finished school, she learned what she needed to know about being a Christian by serving as an apprentice in all the different businesses and departments of Aletheia.

"This is one of my favourite places," she confided to the others. "I could sweep the floor in here all day!" She watched them enter the elevator, and returned to humming and polishing once more.

A man was already inside the elevator when they entered. He carried a big heavy burden on his back; it was an awkward shape and made of sharp, prickly, jagged weights.

"Oh, that's too bad!" Ben exclaimed, as the man, smiling despite his bent back and awful burden, shuffled up to make room for them. "Can we help? Hugo, if you took one side, and if I… ow! It *is* prickly, isn't it?!"

"It's prickly alright," agreed the man. "Some burdens are like that! Usually the burdens of regret and resentment are the worst, and bitterness! *They* can be pretty uncomfortable too! But at least I only need to get it to the Care-Caster Room[6] – think of the poor soul who's been carrying it around for years and has only just let it go!"

"Carrying it for years!" exclaimed Ben. "Why on earth would anyone do that?!"

"That's a good question," said the man. "It does seem strange, doesn't it? Why would anyone choose to hold on to a burden when they could cast it away – as the Bible says?"

Ben was impressed. "Wow! So you throw that burden…"

"Right into the bottom of the Care-Caster!" said the man cheerfully. "Gone for good – unless they choose to grow another one, of course. But if people keep casting care, then it stays away, doesn't it? It doesn't become bigger and bigger like this one!"

"You're a Burden-Bearer, aren't you?" said Josie. "We met one when we were here before!"

The man smiled. He thought it was the best job in the world. "That's exactly what I am! I help to bear other people's burdens, just like the Bible says. 'Bear one another's burdens'!"[10]

"Why would you do that job?" Ben asked frankly.

"It's fulfilling the law of Christ,"[10] said the man simply.

Ben was silent for a while. The whole rapid, stomach-churning, elevator ride passed, for the most part, unnoticed by him, although it was impossible not to observe how high and how far they were travelling. The Burden-Bearer man got off the elevator halfway up and made his way to the Care-Caster Room, staggering cheerfully down the corridor to get rid of the horrible burden. The elevator ride continued for the four students, higher and higher – until all at once it stopped.

They stepped from the elevator onto a glittering gold and silver hallway. Along the corridor, at exact intervals, guards in white and gold uniforms stood silent and watchful. They observed the teenagers curiously, but one glimpse of their golden cards gave the group unfettered access onwards, down the wonderful passageway, to the heavily guarded silver door with delicately carved golden writing.

They had reached Supplication.

CHAPTER 10
THE SUPPLICATION ROOM

Nothing could have prepared the four visitors for the interior of the room named Supplication. They might justifiably have expected a room of gold and silver, containing treasures of untold value; they might have expected pristine and spotless splendour and order, such as the serious guards portrayed; they might have expected *anything* but what was actually within.

Across the impossibly vast space of the Supplication Room, slowly shifting and twisting and turning through all the activity there, was wonderfully fine mist: the type you might see on a fine summer morning. It wasn't eerie or sinister; it didn't feel cold and unfriendly. It was white, and finely transparent, and it glittered like the purest diamonds in the world. Occasionally they glimpsed the colours of the rainbow, glinting and teasing in dazzling array when sudden shafts of light glowed in the 'mist'. Across the entire floor, threaded through the mist, were dozens of busy workers, operating fifteen stations of complex machines. Each of the separate stations was like nothing they had seen – or even imagined – before. It was made up of several odd bits and pieces of machinery – looms and sewing machines and weaving-type structures of every variety and shape and size. Small and large, tall and short, wide and slender, fitting together as only dissimilar but harmonious pieces can fit – in unexpected and fantastic patterns – like an unfinished jigsaw that suddenly makes sense.

The group stood and stared down at the vast sunken chamber before them. The space below them was massive, *enormous*, *gigantic*, stretching far away on every side.

"It's one of our expandable rooms," the young guard inside the door explained, breaking the breathtaking quiet of the room. "We never run out of space here, and recently it's been in great demand – on account of the secret preparations to defeat our enemies."

That didn't make things any clearer. *What was everybody doing?*

Ben remarked, "If it's a *secret* then plenty of people know about it!"

"It's more of a private preparation than a secret," said the guard. He was interested in these young visitors. They hadn't had spectators since the preparation for this very special mission had commenced.

"Preparation for *what?*" asked Hugo, too curious to pretend he knew what was going on.

Exactly what the mission was about, the young guard had not been informed; he only knew enough to do his duty. "Well, for Operation Grey, of course, but I don't know more than that. I dare say you know more than me, since you've been allowed this far, and since you carry gold cards…"

Hugo cleared his throat. "Well… yes, we're here on a, um, fact-finding mission, to do with, um, Operation Grey…"

The guard nodded gravely, choosing to overlook the giggle of the girl who looked like the lad with the auburn hair who seemed to be in charge – so alike they could be twins.

"You don't actually know that, Hugo," she said.

"I've never heard of Operation Grey," Ben remarked, honestly ignorant.

Josie shook her head. "It wasn't in the book I read."

Hugo ignored them. He didn't think it was a good idea to admit how little they knew. "Are we free to look around?" he asked the guard, trying to regain control.

The guard nodded. "Of course. Follow the arrow. Please don't disturb the workers."

They began to descend the wide stairs to the intriguing chamber of unknown, moveable dimensions. On the floor, guiding their feet, was a glittering golden arrow. As they walked, the arrow moved, showing the next step they should take. They descended the last few steps. And then they understood what was perhaps the most curious and wonderful thing of all. The 'mist' wasn't mist at all – or cloud, or haze, or fog, or gas of any sort. What appeared to be vapour was, in fact, many thousands of strands of glorious, glittering thread – finer than strands of gossamer; stronger than the web of the most skilful spider; softer than the silk of a silkworm; of greater value than all the riches in the world. The threads parted as they took the first few steps, following the glittering golden arrow. Fibres wiped gently across their faces, and ran softly through their fingers: never breaking apart.

Then it was clear: the countless strands of astonishing fibres were being woven by the busy weavers and their machines – into the most incredible patchwork covering. The completed pieces were collected by workers who carried them with the utmost care to the largest space of all – a massive assembly area in the middle of the machines. Here they were being pieced together by workers sewing with golden needles.

They stepped carefully around machines, between busy workers – who raised a hand or gave a wave but never spoke or ceased their duties. They followed the golden arrow on and on. In all the vast area of activity, no one was making a sound. They were happy, busy people, but there was no noise, not even from the machines.

The closer they looked, the more details the four visitors could discern. The fifteen large work stations of many different machines were named. They had simple names. Some of the names were positive – such as, Patience, Kindness, Selfless, and Always-Hope. Others were more negative, such as, Not-Jealous, and No-Boasting.

They all sounded vaguely familiar, as if they belonged together.

They paused to watch the intricate workings of the group at the Patience machines. The most impossibly fine lace was being skilfully woven there. Slowly, painstakingly, the workers bent low over the wonderful thread, creating a pattern of incredible beauty and complexity. Their parts of the covering were slow and full of effort.

Others, such as the folk at the cluster of devices which were named No-Pride, wove quickly: a simple, strong, un-fussy design which would be squares of plainness and no consequence within a bigger, far more elaborate design. But these squares would undoubtedly hold the other squares together.

All the component parts were necessary – from the machines which wove humble designs, to those of great delicacy and splendour; from the darker, warmer, practical patterns, to those of transparency and dazzlingly bright loveliness.

At last they reached the final machine. It was stationed apart from the others, and it was creating a covering all of its own. The device was called *Intercessory*, and there was a space for another name upon it.

Within the space, in golden writing, was the name of *Charlie Steady*.

Ben ran his fingers through the strands, wondering what it all meant; pondering the power, the significance of these marvellous threads created by people praying. He pictured Charlie, in all his misery and need; would it hurt to be prepared for the possible rescue of his friend? Clearly the strands at the Intercessory Machine were specifically for Charlie. He pulled at a handful of gold and silver threads – surprised when they came away easily in his hand. He put them hastily in his pocket. They might be needed to rescue Charlie.

They left the Supplication Room at the far end, following the golden arrow which directed them to depart through a different door. They didn't see the young guard again. Before they knew it, they were once more on the glittering corridor along which they had walked what seemed like an age ago. The room they had just seen was so incredible and unusual they knew there was something of critical importance they must learn. A great mission was afoot in Aletheia, and somehow they might get to play a part. They knew, from past adventures, that it was vital to be prepared.

Ben didn't think he had ever kept quiet for so long, when there was so much he wanted to say. But it hadn't felt right to speak in the busy silence of that marvellous room. "I will never, as long as I live, never, ever, ever, see anything like that *ever* again!" he said solemnly.

"I'm not sure about your grammar, Ben, but I think I agree with you!" Josie removed her notepad from her bag and frantically scribbled notes, using the back of her cousin, Hugo, as a convenient desk.

"Incredible, just incredible," said Henrietta, still sounding dazed.

"But are we *sure* we *know* what it all means?" said Hugo, sounding serious and determined.

Josie stopped her scribbling. "I was making a note of the things I noticed before I forgot." She chewed the end of her pencil then tapped it on Hugo's back as she spoke, "The names of all the work stations..."

"I noticed their names too!" Ben said eagerly.

Josie nodded. "Yes, I think I've got them all down here… and I was wondering what they all meant, how they all fit together..."

"Well?" prompted Hugo.

"I think it's what we've been learning at school all term," said Josie. "About love. There were fifteen work stations, and there are fifteen descriptions of love in the verses we learnt from the Bible[11] – 'Love is patient and kind. Love is not jealous, it does not boast, and it is not proud...'"

"'Love is not rude, is not selfish, and does not become angry easily. Love does not remember wrongs done against it. Love is not happy with evil, but is happy with the truth...'" Henrietta joined in.

"'Love patiently accepts all things. It always trusts, always hopes, and always continues strong'," Ben added. He had a very good memory for recitation; he won prizes for learning verses at school.

"'Love never ends'," concluded Hugo.

Henrietta said, "All the machines were creating patches for the same, um, *quilt*." It was hard to think of the glorious covering being woven in the Supplication Room as something as ordinary as a *quilt*; but it was equally hard to think what else to call it.

"So, the entire blanket-thing is made through supplication – which we know is prayer that petitions God for something we really need," mused Hugo.

"Perhaps petitioning God that *love* might be used to overcome our enemies?" suggested Josie.

"Did you notice the Intercessory Machine that had Charlie's name on it?" asked Ben. "Do you think they're also creating a covering just for him?"

Charlie was on all their minds. He was currently a resident of one of Dr Pentone's wards, in the hospital wing of the Academy of Soldiers-of-the-Cross. He was being treated with various ointments and medicines of Care and Kindness, but so far the treatment had limited effect and he continued to be grey and confused. He simply didn't want to be cured – because he appeared to have no notion that there was anything wrong that needed curing.

"I think I remember that the Intercessory is about asking God for something on behalf of someone else – in this case, for *Charlie*," said Josie.

"Did you notice the threads on the Intercessory were named?" asked Henrietta. "I'm not sure how they got there… but there were definitely name tags. I only caught a glimpse of a couple – they kept shifting about – but I definitely saw *Mrs De Voté* on one of the threads in Charlie's blanket!"

Ben was more puzzled than impressed. He had heard of Mrs De Voté's knitted square which was a powerful prayer token, but he had no personal experience of the power of that old lady's prayers the way Henrietta and the others had during the terrifying purple storm.[7] He could only picture a rosy-cheeked old lady who ran the small Faithful shop on a quiet street of the city.

Henrietta tried to explain. "She's a powerful pray-er. Things happen when she prays!"

"Great things," agreed Hugo. "But Henry, I think Mrs De Voté would want you to explain…"

Henrietta sighed. "I know, I know," she said. "Although, I still think there's something special about Mrs De Voté!"

Ben looked between the twins. How were Mrs De Voté's prayers going to help Charlie?

"Mrs De Voté taught us that it's not the person who prays that is important," explained Henrietta. "The power of prayer is all about *Who* we are praying to, not about us who are praying. It's all about how great God is. So, you see, if we ask God to do something in keeping with what the Bible says about Him[12]… well, God can do *anything!*"

Ben nodded. He had long heard the Truth of it, but now he must learn to practise it. He must ask God to help Charlie. No one else could reach his friend and free him from the grey contamination that coated and saturated all of him. Only God could do that.

"I think maybe there's another thing we're meant to learn from this," said Josie, as they began, with reluctance, to retrace their steps to the elevator to depart from the Prayer Academy.

"What are you thinking, Jo?" asked Hugo.

"I think we must learn to put into practice the actions of love – on Charlie, I mean. I think that the reason they are weaving a covering of love, must be because it will defeat, or help to counter, the poison of the Meddlers' lies. You see, little by little it might help to clear away the grey muddle so that Charlie can see his need and be saved."

CHAPTER 11
OPERATION GREY

There were only five people involved in the leadership meetings which followed the discovery of the White-Jacket Meddlers. Captain Steadfast, the Deputy Chief of Aletheia, led the group. Lieutenant Bourne Faithful, Justice Jude Faithful, Dr Theo Pentone, and Chief Judge Steady were the other members. They met with one aim: to plan the destruction of the Rumour Mill. Many others were preparing for the expedition which must take place to achieve this, but only the few now gathered knew the whole plan, and they spent every spare hour working to find out more.

Captain Steadfast was speaking. "Lieutenant Faithful, have our two young scientists discovered anything further regarding the connection between weather patterns and the movement of White-Jacket Meddlers?"

Bourne shook his head. "No, sir," he said. "At least, nothing that gets us any closer to determining the location of the Rumour Mill. They are certainly conscientious in their efforts though." Dusty and Flair spent every spare moment in the Control Room, relentless in their efforts to help defeat Aletheia's enemies.

Captain Steadfast was fleetingly amused. "I heard about the

inadvertent snow storm in the Control Room the other day," he remarked drily.

Bourne Faithful continued, "Dr Pentone and I are in agreement that we may need to implement our… our more dangerous strategy to determine the location of the Rumour Mill."

There was a moment of silence.

Then, "Operation Grey," the Captain said reluctantly. "I know we have prepared for it, but I hoped it would not come to that. Theo? You're reasonably certain Operation Grey is worth the risk?"

Dr Pentone nodded. "From the experiments I have conducted, I'm absolutely certain that the substance infecting Charlie Steady is White-Jacket Meddler poison. The rest of the process is deduction – as you know, this has never been done before. But I am reasonably satisfied that there is so much pollution in Charlie Steady that the Meddlers have inadvertently created a… well, for want of a better description, a *homing signal*. Charlie, in his current state, will be drawn to the Rumour Mill, just as the Meddlers themselves are. In this way, he will act just like a Meddler."

Captain Steadfast nodded grimly. "So, the location of the Rumour Mill, which we felt we were on the verge of discovering when we tracked down the White-Jacket Meddlers…"

"Personally, I begin to doubt whether it has a permanent, fixed location," said Dr Pentone. "It may stay in one place for a period of time, but I suspect the Meddlers know its current location by instinct – because they are drawn there like a magnet – not by geographic knowledge. As we have discovered, the basic formula for Meddler poison in all the many different types of Meddlers, is the same; they would all be drawn to the Rumour Mill. I believe the Rumour Mill can always be found by those who have imbibed a sufficient amount of poison, and I'm almost certain that now includes Charlie."

Charlie's aunt, Sagacia Steady, the Chief Judge, grimly nodded agreement. Her hands were so tightly clasped together that her knuckles were white. "I also hoped it would not come to this. But I agree that Operation Grey may be necessary."

"Justice Faithful? Do you have any comments?" The Captain turned to the youthful, clever judge-in-training, the younger brother of Bourne, and the final member of these select five.

"I think Operation Grey is necessary," said Jude directly. "The work on weather patterns is probably not accurate enough, and likely to take too long. And we must act soon." Then he added, "But I've also been thinking that Operation Grey might be the best hope for Charlie's salvation. By allowing Charlie to go in the direction of the Rumour Mill, we might help him to come face-to-face with what he is – and with his great need for cleansing."

"And, of course, if Charlie comes to understand his need – that he is poisoned – we know that he can be cured through trusting in the Lord Jesus to cleanse him,"[5] agreed Dr Pentone.

There was a moment of silence as they all, once more, considered the plan which might be their best chance of finding and destroying the Rumour Mill. As things stood, poor, grey, confused Charlie Steady might be their only hope. But could Operation Grey be used for Charlie's blessing, as well as for the good of Aletheia?

At last Captain Steadfast said, "What do the chosen students know of Operation Grey?"

"They know none of the details of the operation, sir," said Bourne, "but we have prepared them. They are, of course, being prepared at school, and they have also visited the Prayer Academy and Supplication."

"Good. And our preparations in Supplication?"

"Complete, sir."

"Very well."

There was a pause which no one wanted to fill.

Then, "Proceed with Operation Grey," said the Captain.

The stage was set.

PART 2: THE JOURNEY

CHAPTER 12
THE HONOURABLE MS HAUTEUR

Charlie idly swiped his stick at the head of a vivid yellow daffodil. The fragile leaves scattered in the warm breeze, and Henrietta, who was following close behind, and who had a moment earlier admired the flowers, exclaimed indignantly at the destruction. Charlie merely smirked.

"Leave it, Henry," Hugo said quietly, pulling his twin away from Charlie's swinging stick.

"At least there are plenty more flowers," remarked Ben. He tried to keep positive – even in the face of Charlie's increasingly rude and unreasonable behaviour.

Josie Faithful, the fifth and final companion on this journey, had her notepad balanced in her hand, and somehow avoided Charlie's annoying stick-swinging and scribbled notes even as they walked.

They had all set off from Aletheia in good spirits. The first night they camped on farmland, just east of Aletheia. They washed in a stream, lit a campfire, boiled water for tea, and fried good Aletheian bacon for supper.

Day two had been muddled. They explored farmland, which all looked the same, then, led by Charlie, they detoured towards

Muddled-by-Self – a damp, constantly flooded town on the banks of the River Self. They didn't get very far: the ground was muddy and boggy and they turned back before they reached the town. There was nothing to see, nothing to do, and they pitched their two tents early and camped on open land which appeared to be dry.

This morning, the morning of day three, their excitement at the commencement of their journey had definitely paled into harsh reality. The ground on which they camped was damp, not dry after all; no one had slept particularly well. Henrietta and Josie wanted a hot shower. Hugo snapped and told them not to be so ridiculous. Ben had fried too much bacon the previous morning and there wasn't enough for everyone. Charlie was the most cheerful of the five, at least when he got his own way. He ate all the remaining bacon and watched the others do the clearing up. Personally, he wouldn't have chosen these four classmates as companions – apart from Ben – but he wasn't going to question why the adults in Aletheia had allowed this journey. The main thing was that they were out of Aletheia, on an adventure in the land of Err.

They packed up their tents, and once more Charlie led the way. Now they headed towards the large, prosperous city of Pride. So far, their entire trip had been going gently downwards, and, the closer they got to Pride, the more their descent steepened – towards the lowest point of the land of Err, which was Pride itself.

"We'z nearly zere!" Charlie pointed at a sign which had suddenly come into view. It was a ridiculously large sign to simply announce the name of a place, but the city of Pride did nothing by halves.

"Pride considers itself the capital city of Err," Josie informed them. "I was reading up about the history of this part of Err…"

"Why wouldz you do zat?" asked Charlie disdainfully.

"It's the biggest town in Err, and the people boast that it's the centre of the land, but of course *Aletheia* is really at the centre! But the people of Err don't want to acknowledge the Truth that is Aletheia…"

Charlie whacked his stick at another flower, and missed.

"…Pride is the fastest growing, most popular town in Err, because there's something about the city that appeals to everyone!"

Charlie swiped another daffodil, beheading it neatly and looking provokingly at Henrietta. Henrietta swallowed hard and bit her lip. *Love is patient… remember how patient God is with our failings…* She repeated it over and over in her mind. It had been wonderful to set out on this most important venture into the land of Err, to do something important for Aletheia. But it was a different story when the reality of travelling with poor, infected Charlie was the daily strain of showing love to someone who had become so completely and irritably unlovable!

They paused at the pretentious town sign which boldly stated, '*Pride: The Town for Everyone*'. Underneath the sign was a list of the prizes won by the town, and even quotes from well-known personalities. '*Governor Genie: "Pride is the one town where everyone will feel at home!"*'

Ben commented, "Presumably that means even Meddlers feel at home here!"

Josie was scrutinising a small screen. They were sharing one of the latest smart, voice-activated, mini Mission Detectors supplied by the Academy of Soldiers-of-the-Cross. It was a device Rescuers used in the land of Err. It gave directions, was a source of all sorts of information and useful warnings, and even showed their location in the Central Control Room of Aletheia.

"Pride has won the '*Err in Bloom*' competition for at least eleven years," Josie read from the screen.

"They won't win 'Err in Bloom' this year when they find that Charlie has beheaded all their flowers," muttered Henrietta.

Suddenly, onto the empty road ahead, stepped a smart woman in a completely black uniform – which looked like an extremely well-pressed onesie. She had come from nowhere, and had evidently appeared for *them*. For an official of Err, she had an odd appearance. In fact, so artificial was her appearance that she looked more like a mannequin than a real person: not a hair out of place, and makeup freshly and liberally applied.

"Step this way for inspection!" she commanded in an imperious tone.

Beyond the sign, until now hidden from view, was a single storey structure which was excessively white and clinical in appearance. Outside it, a white sign with black writing on it stated, '*Border Assessment Clinic*'. It appeared more formal and boring than threatening, and, too surprised to do otherwise, the group followed the black clad woman.

"*Assessment Clinic* makes it sound as if they might check us for head lice," remarked Ben in an undertone.

Josie was frantically pressing buttons on the small Mission Detector, wishing they had been more thorough in their investigation of the rules for entering Pride. But they had no idea that Charlie would head to Pride, and how could they have guessed that they would have to be assessed to enter the town? As far as Josie was previously aware, places in Err were free to enter – even though she knew they could sometimes be tricky to leave.[13]

There was a straight white line painted across the road – from the Border Assessment Clinic to a high, spiky fence. Josie lagged behind the others being marched to the clinic by the artificial-looking woman, reading words which were appearing on the small Mission Detector she held in her hand: *'The white line, which marks the border of Pride, appears harmless enough, but it is not wise to cross it without the precaution of…'* She didn't have time to read what they might need to cross that line. Was the protection of their armour of God[3] sufficient to cross it? Or must they enter through the Border Assessment Clinic instead?

Meanwhile, Henrietta, intrigued by the border guard woman, endeavoured to read her badge as they entered the clinic. There were plenty of words. Eventually she read, *'The Honourable Ms Hauteur: Deputy Assistant to Lead Qualified Border Assessor, Border Access and Control, City of Pride.'*

Seriously? They needed all those words to say… what exactly? That Ms Hauteur was a border-guard-cum-assistant who wasn't even qualified? And *'The Honourable'*…? Were *all* the people titled here?

Ms Hauteur was neither friendly nor amenable to visitors entering Pride. She seemed distinctly unimpressed with the group who were now on her territory. They were certainly not as immaculate as she. They stood in a row, feeling sheepish, scanning the large, white, barren room of the Assessment Clinic. Almost the only furniture were stark white chairs, fixed to the floor. The only other thing of note was a strange, shining curtain that obscured whatever lay beyond.

Ms Hauteur addressed them formally, reading from a piece of paper. "If you are carrying disease, termites, communicable conditions, contagious illnesses, unpleasant odours, infectious warts, oozing pimples, and other such unpleasantries, you will be further processed at Quarantine Quality Control." She gestured through the wide window to where a white, distinctly clinical-looking building was hiding behind distant trees, looking frighteningly like an institution of no-return. "If you suffer from mind conditions, such as Humblepieous, Selfdisdainia, Meekocia, Obsequiousnessness, and similar, you will be recommended treatment. If you are untidy, scruffy, unclean, slovenly, un-matching, ill-fitting, and otherwise generally not up to our standards, you will be…"

Hugo felt it was time to move on. "Uh, right," he said. "We really just want to travel through Pride, um, your Honourable…"

Henrietta choked over a giggle at his choice of address, which drew the ice-cold glare of Ms Hauteur. Hugo glared at her too. Now was not the time to get on the wrong side of the border agent, and, although this scene was utterly ridiculous, it was also increasingly concerning. They must get on their journey.

Hugo tried to be as polite as possible. "If you wouldn't mind doing the assessment or whatever it is…"

Ms Hauteur did not like to be interrupted in her relishing account of the list of undesirable things the city of Pride enjoyed treating and eradicating. She looked coldly at Hugo and the others. "Do you understand the disclaimer of the city of Pride?" she demanded.

"No, not really, although Jo might have read about it," said Ben, who was always honest and who had never heard of *the disclaimer of the city of Pride*. Josie shook her head vigorously. "Well, anyway, we don't care about that bit, you see? We only want to get on our journey…"

Ms Hauteur now had a disagreeable smile fixed on her face. Henrietta imagined it was the way she might look if she was about to squash a nasty bug that she'd just chased all over the house and finally cornered.

"Step this way," she snapped.

Nervously, four of the five stepped forward, looking anxiously at the fifth – at Charlie who was still gazing around him. It never occurred to them that they would fail whatever assessment they had to face: but the awful grey untidiness of Charlie could surely not go unnoticed here; not when they were so fussy about every jolly thing imaginable.

"What doz we need to be inzpected for?" asked Charlie rudely. "Zere'z nothing wrong wiz *me*!"

The Honourable Ms Hauteur turned slowly to the boy she had not particularly noticed until now. Astonishingly, she suddenly seemed impressed. "I like your accent!" she said.

CHAPTER 13
THE POWER OF LOVE

Inside the Academy of Solders-of-the-Cross, the small, select group of people who were responsible for Operation Grey met around a too-large table. They huddled like comrades at one end of the table, close and confiding.

As usual, Captain Steadfast chaired the meeting. "I understand Operation Grey has now reached the town of Pride?"

"Pride, you say? They've definitely reached the boundary?" Dr Theo Pentone leaned forward, his elbows on the table. "Pride…yes, that's very interesting, and not wholly unexpected…" He sank back in his seat again, lost in thought.

Dusty sat forward on the edge of his seat, enjoying his informal inclusion at this meeting. He had only appeared to bring Jude the latest report from Josie, but Jude had generously waved him to a seat.

"Um, why do you think they're heading for Pride, sir?" Dusty asked in the convenient pause. Dr Pentone, to whom he directed the question, was still deep in thought and appeared to be almost dozing. But he sat up at once at Dusty's question.

"Pride is at the root of much that is wrong in us," he said. "It was the cause of the fall of mankind in the Garden of Eden.[14] It is still the cause of sin and is most certainly one of the foundation stones of lies and slander! What are lies but a form of pride – a way of promoting or protecting ourselves at the expense of, or instead of, others? If we exaggerate truth, it becomes a lie – it is merely pride and boasting. If we hide a wrongdoing behind a lie – it is only our pride protecting ourselves. If we speak a lie against somebody else – it is simply to raise our interests higher than others. If we cheat and defraud – it is solely to better ourselves or protect our own interests. The Bible teaches us that there is nothing good about us whatsoever,[15] but the city of Pride promotes the ultimate lie: that we are alright after all, and we can take pride in what the Bible has condemned. Pride, *Pride* is the first place *I* would search for those lying, delinquent rascals!"

"Oh, I see," said Dusty, rather feebly, unsure that he did, in fact, understand.

Captain Steadfast returned to the matter in hand. "Lieutenant Faithful is still closely shadowing the operation?" It was a question to which they all knew the answer; but it was comforting to hear it nonetheless.

Justice Jude Faithful nodded. "Yes, sir." His brother, Bourne, would stick like glue to those five students. He would be concealed somewhere close by with his group of hand-picked Rescuers, watching, observing, ready to rush in. And he had the backup of the forces of

Aletheia just a call away.

"What is the update on the condition of Charlie Steady?"

Jude flicked through the reports he had received from Dusty. The update on Charlie was a colourfully detailed record kept by Jude's meticulous sister, Josie. "Josie reports that Charlie continues to be grey in colour. He isn't always able to distinguish the truth from a lie and continues to be completely self-deceived; he has no idea of his grey appearance. He still has the Meddlers' accent…" Jude quickly scanned other paragraphs of Josie's report, wishing his sister had summarised more, and described less. "Practising the actions of love is proving challenging…"

"Yes, it usually is," agreed Dr Pentone. "But we have very clear instructions from the Bible how we should show love. The coming of the Lord Jesus into the world introduced a new type of love. This love isn't offered because something is nice or lovable, but is entirely dependent on the person who loves. You just decide to love because God commanded it – you don't expect anything in return. It is not the value of the object which determines love, but the determination of love itself!"

Dusty had never thought about that before – but how very reassuring it was that the love of God was rooted in His determined will to set His great love upon people and seek their good – without anything about them being remotely lovable. He remembered a verse he had learned about how God demonstrated how much He loved the world – through sending the Lord Jesus Christ to die for people when they were at their most unlovable and very worst – *when we were still sinners.*[16] It was comforting to know that even now, when he, Dusty, was at his very worst, God's love was still fixed upon him. Nothing could change that.

Jude was continuing to scan the report. He added, "Josie has given some examples of the actions of love which appear to have taken the edge off the greyness and relieved Charlie's muddled mind, even if only temporarily."

Chief Judge Sagacia Steady removed her spectacles and rubbed her tired eyes. These were trying days for any member of Charlie's family. "But at least that will give Charlie an opening to see the Truth!" she said.

"Continuing to show Charlie patience and kindness, forgiving him for his ongoing unreasonableness and rudeness, and so on... there's quite a lot of information here... but the upshot is that acting in love has, indeed, removed some of the grey from his face and hair, and allowed his mind to clear at times."

"Better than my medicines!" exclaimed Dr Pentone. "Pure love, as the Bible describes it, is the least understood and most underrated thing in the entire land of Err! If the members of Operation Grey can continue to demonstrate the actions of love to Charlie, they are his best hope of coming to realise how great the love of God is!"

Dusty wished he dared to interrupt and ask more questions. Was the power of love enough to counter the poisonous lies of the Meddlers which had smothered Charlie? Would this release his mind from bondage and flood it with the light of the message of God's great salvation? Dusty knew there was a cure for every sin and wrong, because the Lord Jesus had defeated the ultimate consequence of sin – death – at the cross. There was no wrong that the Bible could not deal with![5] But how could the power of love – however it was used – possibly be strong enough to overcome something as evil as the Rumour Mill?

CHAPTER 14
THE VANITOR'S ASSESSMENT

As unlikely though it seemed, there was no doubt that the border guard, *The Honourable* Ms Hauteur, approved of Charlie Steady. It was unclear whether she even noticed the dirty, grey substance that begrimed him. From the moment he had spoken, in the awful, harsh accent which marked him like one of the Meddlers, she had seen – or heard – something in him to which she could relate, and which she evidently felt was wanting in the others.

"Wait here," she snapped at the other four. Then to Charlie, "Now, young man, you take your place here and we'll see what can be done for you."

Charlie, seeing nothing unusual in being given preferential treatment – in fact, considering it his right – took his place. From being indignant and rude and rebellious, he was suddenly surprisingly compliant.

Hugo watched the proceedings with growing dread. Whatever was going on here, it was no good thing that this Ms Hauteur admired Charlie's accent and saw nothing wrong with him. If she couldn't see error, then she was certainly not aware of Truth.

Ms Hauteur temporarily disappeared through the shimmering

curtain which hid a section of the clinic. Hugo watched the curtain warily. Whatever it concealed, it was certain to be another hindrance they did not want. He began to wonder about sounding the secret emergency code to summon Bourne Faithful and his band of Rescuers who were somewhere close by, shadowing them.

"Why is she called *The Honourable?*" hissed Ben.

"Certainly not because she is *honourable!*" retorted Henrietta in a fierce whisper.

"In Pride, people like to have titles," Josie explained in an undertone, having learnt this from the Mission Detector. "*The Honourable* is actually one of the lowest titles. She can only become a Lady, or Baroness, or Marchioness, or Countess, or Viscountess, or Duchess or some other such thing by getting promoted or doing something great for the town of Pride."

"That's nuts," Ben said frankly. He had never dreamt of attaining a title of any kind.

Ms Hauteur reappeared from behind the glimmering curtain – accompanied by the most surprising companion. It was a 'creature' that none of them had ever seen in real life – although they were aware of such things. It was a Vanitor.

Vanitors were an invention of Pride. They were robots – intended to carry out menial tasks for people. Their appearance was strange:

you could not easily see what a Vanitor looked like because it was clothed in mirrors; it simply reflected what it saw. But a Vanitor didn't only reflect its surroundings, it improved them too. If an object was shining, it was even brighter in a Vanitor's reflection; if it was dull, it showed lustre; if it was small, it became big; if it was plain, it looked beautiful. The people of Pride loved Vanitors because they were the best reflection of themselves they could hope to have.

People who lived in Pride could no longer remember a time when Vanitors were not a part of their everyday lives. And, since their invention, the city of Pride spent a large portion of their wealth on the development of the curious robot-type-creature. But no matter how much was invested, they were still metallic and clumsy, not beautiful at all. There was an ever-expanding array of Vanitor accessories made available to help beautify them – clothes, wigs, hats, gloves, jewellery, bags, shoes, boots, and so on. There was never any problem at Christmas knowing what to buy someone from Pride – there was no end to what people would purchase for their pets, and no end to the tasks the Vanitors were now being asked to perform.

The group from Aletheia had seen pictures of Vanitors but they had never encountered one close up, far less been examined by one.

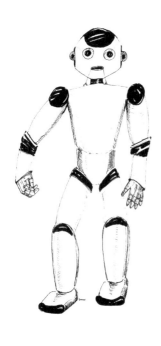

The Vanitor walked awkwardly on its steel legs to where Charlie stood, his feet placed squarely on the white painted feet marks on the floor. Its unblinking robot eyes stared at Charlie. "My name is Vernon," it intoned in a cold, mechanical voice.

"At least it's not *The Honourable* Vernon!" whispered Ben to Henrietta.

The voice continued. "I am your Border Assessor today. We hope that you love yourself. Please wait while I assess your state."

"It's politer than Honourable Haughty Hauteur!" Henrietta whispered back to Ben.

Josie and Hugo were both glaring at the other two. Now was *not* the time to hinder their journey by giving Ms Hauteur an excuse to detain them. For all they knew she could hold them here indefinitely – or perhaps even refuse them entry to Pride altogether.

Charlie stared disdainfully at the small, unblinking robot. "Azzezz *my ztate!*" he exclaimed. "Zerez nothing wrong wiz my ztate!"

"That is a correct answer," said Vernon mechanically.

Ben and Henrietta stared at each other. But thankfully, to the relief of Hugo and Josie, they were too surprised to speak. This was weirder and weirder!

Vernon the Vanitor's head moved up and down in an odd sequence of clicks and clacks, as he – or *it* – began a slow circle of examination, examining Charlie's feet, hands, and, most eerily, reaching its claw-like mechanical fingers and touching the area over his heart. "Unknown substance coating Traveller. Substance acceptable under City Ordinance 194…"

Josie wished she could write all this down. She *must* get to grips with the recording device on the Mission Detector! Dusty and Flair would want to know every word. But it took very little analysis to understand that, if the assessment of Pride found the grey-coating of Meddlers' poisonous lies and slander acceptable, then they must be heading in the right direction for the Rumour Mill. How strange that the home of lies could be close to somewhere as posh and fussy as the town of Pride!

Ms Hauteur appeared unsurprised at the Vanitor's assessment and nodded her approval. Charlie's assessment was concluded with no other controversial findings or recommendations. Not a word about his uncombed hair, or untucked T-shirt, or the fact that he had only washed in a stream for the past three days, or about the mud on his shoes. All appeared to be concealed under the grey substance of which the city of Pride *approved*. That which was such a problem for Charlie's friends from Aletheia, was more than acceptable here.

"Jo!" whispered Henrietta frantically, unable to help herself. "Do you see in the mirrors…?!"

"I see it," Josie whispered softly in return.

In the shining reflection of the Vanitor's skin, the grey matter which coated Charlie became beautiful and was wonderfully glistening.

"Entry approved." That was the Vanitor's final verdict on Charlie. Then it bumbled away and stood to one side, its unblinking gaze turned upon the other four who awaited their turn.

Ms Hauteur smiled a sickly sort of smile. There were no kind smile-wrinkles around her eyes or mouth; her smile was unfeeling and immobile. "You are cleared for entry, young man," she said to Charlie. "Congratulations! Straight to the door at the end, and you're in Pride! Transport will take you to the city centre…"

Charlie glanced at his companions. He looked smug.

"Charlie! Wait!" exclaimed Hugo, horrified at the thought of losing sight of Charlie at this critical juncture. They had faithfully promised *never* to let him out of their sight!

Ms Hauteur turned a thoroughly nasty stare on Hugo. "You wait here!" she commanded. "Your friend is cleared for entry. *You* will now undergo assessment!"

Charlie took a step to the door which led to the other side of the white boundary line – into the territory of Pride.

"Charlie!" called Ben. "Wait a moment, we'll be with you soon…!"

Charlie shrugged. "What'z zee big deal?" he said. "I'z juzt be waiting outzide."

Ms Hauteur was now ushering him along.

"Zee you zoon!" said Charlie.

And, just like that, he vanished from their sight.

CHAPTER 15
ACCESS DENIED!

With a feeling of grim foreboding, Hugo took his place on the painted white feet to undergo the Vanitor's assessment. At first, he had thought they would have nothing to fear from the assessment of Pride; it was the state of Charlie that had worried him. But since Charlie had been approved for entry, he wondered whether the rest of them, dressed in their protective armour of God,[3] would be found inadequate – and perhaps recommended for ridiculous treatment to meet the city of Pride's standards. Whatever happened, it must happen fast. They must get through this assessment and go after Charlie before they lost him for good!

Ms Hauteur grew increasingly obnoxious. It was as if she had taken the plastic mask off her rigid, perfectly made-up face – and revealed something ugly and terrible beneath.

"Remove your rucksack," she commanded Hugo. She eyed the rucksack with avid attention. And yet it was a neat and tidy enough rucksack – plain and dark and of no special interest at all.

Most reluctantly, Hugo handed his precious rucksack to Ben – not that he didn't trust Ben, but they all had their own burdens to carry on this journey, and they had promised not to let them go. That was two promises which were suddenly in jeopardy: they had lost sight of Charlie, and now he had let go of his rucksack – the contents of which were valuable indeed. Ben clutched the rucksack tightly, giving Hugo a reassuring nod.

Ms Hauteur watched carefully. It was peculiar, the interest she took in the unremarkable rucksack.

The assessment commenced. The cold, mechanical, clawed hands of the unblinking Vanitor reached and touched Hugo.

Immediately there was the most terrific commotion!

EEEWWWOO…EEEWWWOO…EEEWWWOO…

The harsh, ear-splitting alarm vibrated around the border clinic. Something was very, very wrong. Vernon the Vanitor began to turn in frantic circles. One touch of Hugo and he had gone completely mad!

Ms Hauteur was the only one present who didn't seem surprised, and who didn't even seem to mind the horrible noise. "Alright, alright…" She pointed a remote control at the Vanitor and pressed a button. There was sudden, unearthly silence and Vernon stopped dead, his robot face caught in the middle of a blink – which made him look bewildered and absurd.

Ms Hauteur calmly lifted the lid from the top of the Vanitor's head and peered inside. She twiddled with a couple of knobs and

Vernon blinked eerily and unhappily. She replaced the cap. Vernon blinked once more, managing to appear chastened and mortified at the intervention. "Assessment," commanded Ms Hauteur.

"Unknown protection coating Traveller…" That bit was oddly similar to Charlie's assessment. But there the comparison ended.

"Illegal substance: protection against pride, conceit, self, vanity…"

"Enough!" Ms Hauteur's voice rose shrilly in anger. The Vanitor stopped immediately.

"It's detecting the protection of the armour of God!" whispered Josie to herself.

Ms Hauteur scrutinised Hugo. He was taller than she was, but she made him feel very small. "I thought so," she said, relishing the moment. "Region 15, is it?"

"Region 15?" For a moment Hugo forgot that *Region 15* was the name the land of Err gave to Aletheia. Things had taken a very peculiar turn and were rapidly becoming out of control. He had a sick feeling in the pit of his stomach: suddenly he knew that they were on the brink of losing everything they were fighting for on this journey.

"You *are* a Traveller from Region 15?" Ms Hauteur enquired coldly.

"I'm from the city of Aletheia," Hugo replied firmly.

Ms Hauteur sniggered. "I don't know I'd be as quick to claim that these days," she said. "What with your Chief being found to be corrupt…"

"What?!" Henrietta was outraged.

"Henry…" Josie snagged her arm.

Ms Hauteur merely smiled. "Didn't you know, dear?" she purred nastily. "Didn't you know that your Chief has a box in the Bank of Err filled with pilfered treasures from your beloved city? It's all been found out; there's no use denying it!"

Ben had had enough. "Certainly no use discussing it with *you* anyway," he said in disgust. "I don't think you'd know the Truth if it hit you on the head!"

"I'm not sure that's helpful, Ben," muttered Josie helplessly.

Ms Hauteur wasn't bothered. "Loyal Aletheians," she mocked. "Come to be re-made in Pride!"

"We wouldn't want *Pride* to make us anything!" Ben no longer cared what this horrible, plastic woman thought. It was pretty clear they were in trouble with her anyway.

From coldly mocking, Ms Hauteur turned rapidly to snarling. "*Access denied!*" she yelled shrilly at the four stupefied Aletheians.

"I think we already knew that!" exclaimed Ben angrily in return.

Ms Hauteur no longer took any notice of them. "I'll get promotion for discovering this," she mumbled to herself, suddenly speeding for the shimmering curtain. "I'll be a *Lady* at last, maybe a better border post…"

As soon as Ms Hauteur vanished from view, several things happened.

Hugo stepped from the painted white feet. "Ben…!" he began urgently.

When Hugo moved, Vernon the Vanitor began the harsh alarm again and, eerily, horrifyingly, the robot's mechanical hands began to extend towards all four of them – preparing to embrace them in a horrible metal cage. They felt a strange, unwelcome force holding them rooted to the spot. They were not going to be able to escape!

Ben quickly handed Hugo his precious rucksack.

"Any ideas?" Hugo secured his rucksack on his back.

"We have to get out of here…!"

Josie cupped her hands over her ears to protect them from the awful noise. "Let me think!"

Suddenly Ben cried, "Our golden cards from the Prayer Academy…!" And with the swift thought came lightning-quick action. As the Vanitor's terrifying metal arms began to change direction and make a pen to close them in, Ben reached for his precious golden card and flung it at the Vanitor's head. He was a very good shot, but even he couldn't have anticipated the incredible result.

With a terrific CRASH, Vernon's head flew clean off his body and smashed through the window. Simultaneously, whatever invisible force was pinning them in place vanished.

"Nice one, Ben!" shouted Hugo.

The unhappy Vanitor's body lay smashed and useless on the ground. The long metal arms which would have been their cage were no more threatening than the crushed legs of a long-dead spider. The cogs and wheels, and buttons and keys – all the tiny metal components of the Vanitor (apart from its head!) – lay strewn around the once tidy Border Assessment Clinic.

There were noises from beyond the curtain. Only seconds had passed, and they wondered whether Ms Hauteur, whom they assumed was calling for back-up to deal with them, had had a chance to make her call. Whatever the case, she would shortly reappear – and they must be gone.

"To the door!" yelled Hugo.

They rushed for the exit through which Charlie had vanished. No force field or other mischief withstood them, and they crashed through the door and out into the sunshine, free! They had crossed the boundary. Now they were in the territory of Pride.

Ben glanced back as they ran down the road. Was there any chance Charlie was loitering outside the clinic building, still waiting for them? But all that could be seen was the sunshine glinting incongruously on the still blinking eye in the severed head of the unfortunate Vanitor.

They heard the shrill shout of Ms Hauteur and dived under the cover of the thick trees that grew at the side of the road and screened the repulsive 'Quarantine Quality Control' building of Pride.

Now they must decide what should be done.

Most importantly: *where was Charlie?*

CHAPTER 16
FOR THE GREATER GOOD

There was no time to waste. Hugo had a Remote Talker in his hand. "Discovered…" was all he had time to say in his hasty call to Lieutenant Bourne Faithful. Then a piercing whistle split the air, and the high-pitched yell of Ms Hauteur closed in on them.

They started to run. It was not particularly easy to move at speed through the dense, unfriendly wood which bordered the road. These were strange trees – growing large prickles rather than twigs and branches; a barrier, not pleasant woodland. They kept glimpsing the white walls of the extensive Quarantine Quality Control building. It looked like the worst kind of hospital – more like a prison than a place of treatment and remedy. It appeared that the prickly trees were intended to prevent the people in Quarantine Control from escaping, but they were impeding the Aletheians' progress too.

Soon there were other shouts besides the shrill, angry tones of Ms Hauteur. Judging by the sounds, they had at least a dozen border guards on their heels, and there was the deep-throated bark of big dogs picking up their scent.

The four teenagers stopped and looked at each other. They knew.

There was only one reason they had attracted such an interested and venomous response from Ms Hauteur; there was only one reason they would be of such interest to so many border guards of Pride.

Ben said it first. "Hauteur spotted it, didn't she?" His usually cheerful countenance was tense and exceedingly pale.

"Yes," said Hugo. "She's smarter than she looked, and I think she did sense it, maybe even from the start. We should never have followed her into that assessment clinic…"

"I should have read the Mission Detector's advice on crossing the border," Josie said regretfully. "I just never imagined…"

Henrietta looked pretty sick. "Well, we didn't know, and it's done now."

Hugo stared at his sister. "I'm sorry, Henry," he said gruffly. "I never thought it would come to this…" His voice wobbled a bit.

"It's alright, Hugo," Henrietta squared her shoulders valiantly. "We have to do it, to protect it, for the greater good. Quickly."

From the rucksack he carried, Hugo removed another rucksack – neatly folded – identical to the one he carried. He shook it out hastily, and deftly Henrietta placed her own, slightly smaller, rucksack inside it. Then she strapped it on her back. It looked in every way identical to the rucksack that Hugo carried. She kissed her brother on the cheek – and for once he didn't protest. Ben patted her awkwardly on the back. Josie wrapped her arms around her cousin and tried to control her tears.

Hugo said two more words on the Remote Talker, hoping they would reach his commander Bourne Faithful. "Plan Henry," was all he said.

The sounds of baying dogs and shouting guards penetrated the thick forest.

"Quickly!" urged Henrietta. "They're coming!"

Without another word, Hugo, Ben and Josie melted into the trees.

Henrietta was left alone: a willing sacrifice for the greater good.

"*Plan Henry*? You mean to say that Henrietta Wallop was taken?" Captain Steadfast's elbows were leaning heavily on the large table in the nearly empty meeting room. His hands were fisted tightly together and he cracked his knuckles, making Sagacia Steady cringe.

"It was one of a series of plans we had in place for contingencies." Lieutenant Bourne Faithful stood almost to attention.

His brother had taken a seat at the table, but now Jude began to pace the room. Dr Pentone was already pacing up and down like a caged animal. Only the sober Judge sat at the table with the Captain, outwardly calm, except that her hands moved nervously and she fiddled with a ring on her finger.

"The border guards suspected what they carried?"

"As we were aware might happen, something penetrated the disguise and aroused the suspicions of the guard on duty – a Ms *Hauteur*, I believe. She raised the general alarm and the border forces went after them."

"We hoped they might enter unnoticed," muttered the Captain regretfully.

Bourne braced himself to deliver further bad news. "We have traced Henrietta to the quarantine facility across Pride's border."

The Captain's big fist smashed onto the table. It wasn't that he was angry with his most reliable Lieutenant, but he was furious with the meddling of Pride. The Quarantine Quality Control buildings of Pride were almost inaccessible. "What protection does she have with her?"

"The whole armour of God.[3] Nothing else."

"It was essential for her not to carry anything that those slippery border agents could find and investigate." Dr Pentone came away from the window he was scowling at and suddenly strolled towards the table.

"I take it these *contingency* plans have had your input too, Theo?" Captain Steadfast asked warily.

Dr Pentone nodded. "Remember, she willingly sacrificed herself – for the good of Charlie. *'Love does not seek its own'*."[11]

"You mean, I suppose, that Henrietta's action will have a further, positive effect for Charlie's good?" asked Sagacia.

"Precisely," said the doctor.

Captain Steadfast cracked his knuckles again. "Operation Grey was always going to be risky," he said wearily. "But I would like to get my hands on those guards at that quarantine centre…!"

"After me, sir," Lieutenant Faithful said stiffly.

"If I may, sir," Jude scanned a report he had received from Dusty just before he rushed to the meeting. "It seems that perhaps Henrietta's sacrifice is already yielding positive results for Charlie. In some way the love that he was shown has had an effect on him, and the other three, who are going after him, are receiving a faint signal on the Mission Detector they carry. For now, they can track him."

"Excellent!" Dr Pentone rubbed his hands. "We are creating our own homing signal to rival the Meddlers! I don't believe that's ever been done before! And such a sacrifice on the part of Miss Wallop will hopefully give them a good enough signal to discover the boy!"

"Let's hope they find him before…"

"Yes, sir," said Jude.

Captain Steadfast didn't need to complete his thought. They all knew that if the three remaining teenagers didn't find Charlie and continue with their endeavours to show him love, he might arrive at the Rumour Mill without them. Then they might never be able to reach him and bring him back again.

"Prayer cover?" asked Captain Steadfast.

"Strong, sir," reported Jude.

"Excellent. Keep prayer continuing."

"Sir…?" Lieutenant Faithful waited for dismissal. He must get back to his group of hand-picked followers. They were all the best Rescuers he could find, and he did not doubt their ability. But he would not rest while those five teenagers were now scattered across the dangerous territory of Pride.

Jude picked up his papers and prepared to leave the meeting room after the others. He glanced once more through the reports. Somehow his sister had managed to send a comprehensive verbal report via the small Mission Detector as they made their way after Charlie. Dusty had turned that into a written report, and there was a small detail Jude had not noticed during the meeting. There was one more thing that Henrietta had been carrying when she was taken. Josie reported that she had in her pocket her golden card from the Prayer Academy.

Jude managed to smile as he left the meeting room. Things might not be quite as dark for Henry after all.

CHAPTER 17
CHARLIE, HOITY, AND TOITY

Charlie was delighted with his drive through the city of Pride. He wasn't sure how it had happened, but he found himself aboard an immaculate, luxurious Atob, escorted by a distinguished border guard named Baron Hoity. The guard was waiting outside the clinic door. Charlie tried to tell the guard that he was waiting for his friends, but Baron Hoity didn't listen. He reassured Charlie that his friends would soon follow him, so Charlie climbed onto the comfy sofa which stretched along the back of the Atob. He was most impressed by how helpful everyone was.

An Atob was simply a vehicle for getting from A to B. It wasn't the best on long, arduous journeys, but in good weather, for short rides, it was a great way to travel. It was open at the sides, with a fabric shade above. The driver and front passenger faced forward, and the other seats faced backwards. The seats were padded armchairs or cushioned sofas. The Atobs of Pride lacked no comfort; they were the very best.

Charlie's drive through the city streets, in an important 'official' Atob, left nothing to be desired. He sat at the back of the three-wheeled vehicle, being chauffeur-driven by Baron Hoity, feeling like a prince of Pride. The only incongruous part of this splendid taxi ride was the Vanitor, whom Baron Hoity introduced as Toity, and who occupied the front passenger seat. It was the oddest tour guide you could possibly imagine. In a mechanical voice, Toity, the Vanitor, gave a running commentary on everything they were passing.

"Sorry about Toity's accent," Baron Hoity said regretfully. "We're working on improvements, but he still doesn't sound enough like me!"

"Zat'z OK," said Charlie. He spread himself out on the large, comfy sofa, enjoying the view from the back of the vehicle. It was great to be riding instead of walking; it was nice to feel the warm breeze across his face.

"Houses in Pride are made of the best materials in Err," remarked Toity.

Charlie gaped at the houses which lined the streets through which they drove. It wasn't the materials – whatever they were – that he was interested in – it was the *lack* of materials which was remarkable. Whole sections of the front of houses were see-through – so you could see inside the parts of the houses that people were most proud of. Some houses showcased entire floors or sections. The more a house had to be proud of, the more a house showed off. It was a mark of success to have a see-through house. In one room, Charlie could see a small robot-Vanitor dusting dozens of gleaming trophies in a cabinet; in another, an artist painted a large picture which was facing the road – so you could see precisely what was being created. The painting made no sense – a weird splattering of paint spread wildly and randomly over a canvas – but the artist was proud of it anyway.

Charlie could have looked for hours into people's homes – particularly as they were so splendid. He didn't take any notice of the ugly cracks which had appeared in places across some of the walls and roofs. Pride built for style, not substance, and many households had spent their money on appearance instead of important things like foundations.

But there were so many other things to see besides the houses. The trees!

"Zee treez are different colourz here!" exclaimed Charlie, cutting across Toity's monotonous commentary on building methods in Pride.

"Say something about trees, Toity," commanded Baron Hoity.

"Current tree-trend: trees painted rainbow shades…"

The trees were certainly all the colours of the rainbow. The trunks glowed red, orange, yellow, green, blue, indigo, and violet. The leaves sparkled with glitter in the same shades. Around and about the trees, workers were busy collecting stray leaves, and touching up the colours where there was the least evidence of nature taking control.

"There are 1972 trees in Pride. 13.7% of annual city budget spent on tree painting…"

"Are zee flowerz…?"

"Say something about the flowers, Toity," commanded Hoity, cutting across the Vanitor's continuing comments on paint factories, and past, present, and future trends in tree types and colours. Pastel shades were to be introduced next year…

"Flowers first manufactured in Pride in year 2000. Scent added during production. 90% of flowers in Pride: synthetic. 11.9% of annual city budget spent…"

"They'z not even real!" exclaimed Charlie. He had a fleeting recollection of the flowers he had destroyed on their journey, and of Henry's disappointment – and yet her *kindness* to him too, despite what he had done. It was an unsettling feeling. Suddenly the sights and wonders they were passing seemed less splendid: like a smooth façade covering a stinking and rotten inside.

That was when he spotted the big hole. It was surrounded by a painted barrier depicting lovely homes and happy, smiling people; but he caught a glimpse of what the covering was intended to hide. It was a massive sinkhole, into which a large mansion had tumbled. All that remained was the mess of a broken home.

"Look at zat hole!" exclaimed Charlie.

"Sinkholes are prominent in Pride. Growing problem…"

"Shut up, Toity!" snapped Hoity. "We don't tell visitors about sinkholes!"

Charlie had a memory stirring in his clouded mind. Verses he had been taught as a child in Aletheia. One about '*Pride goes before destruction, and a haughty spirit before a fall…*'[17]

There were numerous shops and restaurants in the commercial district. There were plenty of other official tour Atobs too, with Vanitors in the front passenger seat waving their mechanical arms around and giving the same commentary that Charlie was listening to. There were an inordinate number of shops selling trophies, and cups, and rosettes, and framed certificates, and other types of prizes. Charlie could not help but wonder if a trophy was of any real value if anyone could buy one in the local shop.

Toity commented on the metals and materials used in the so-called *Gilded Industry* of Pride which produced the thousands of trophies and prizes the citizens of Pride collected.

People on the streets all had Vanitors following them. The Vanitors carried shopping bags, cups of coffee and trays of food, and various other burdens for their owners; a couple were even walking dogs. As the Atob passed, one Vanitor was picking up dog's mess and putting it into a plastic bag. The strange little robots were glinting in the bright sunlight as their mirrors showed enhanced images of everything they reflected. Many of them had touches of colour too – a bag, a hat, jewellery, and other miscellaneous things – which generally matched what their owners wore.

"Say something about Personal Vanitors, Toity," commanded Hoity, bored of endless facts about metals and materials and manufacturing methods used in the booming Gilded Industry of Pride.

"99.99% of people in Pride own a Personal Vanitor," said Toity.

"Who'z doezn't have onez?" asked Charlie, amused that someone, somewhere was daring to be different. He didn't expect an answer, but:

"No Vanitor allowed in Humbie House," intoned Toity.

"Humbie Houze? What'z zat?" asked Charlie. He wasn't sure why, but the mention of that name struck a chord deep inside. It was a weird feeling and it came out of nowhere. It was like a suppressed memory which was unpleasant – but was so important that it must be remembered.

"Humbie House has unknown origins; declared illegal in 1969; breach of City Ordinances 1, 2, 3, 4, 5, 6, 7…"

"Enough!" snapped Hoity.

Toity was immediately silent, his head drooping, as if he felt sad at the rebuke.

"They're in breach of every relevant City Ordinance," Baron Hoity explained. "Toity will go on reeling off numbers all day! They should have programmed the Tour Vanitors to summarise more, and he has no jokes whatsoever!"

"What haz Humbie Houze done?" asked Charlie, intrigued about this unknown place without understanding why. What was tugging his mind there, despite the fact that it was illegal and had broken all the Ordinances of this splendid city…?

Baron Hoity shrugged. "No one visits Humbie," he said dismissively. "The City Council is considering options for demolition."

For reasons he could not understand, Charlie felt unaccountably sad that the place called Humbie House might be demolished.

"This is the end of our tour," Baron Hoity pulled the Atob to a halt beside the magnificent sparkling fountain which was the centrepiece of Pride – situated at the heart of the immaculate, sumptuous city square. "Drink from the water," he directed. "That will make your stay in Pride more meaningful."

"We hope you enjoyed your ride today," intoned Toity. "Further information about Pride is found at…"

Charlie stepped from his comfy sofa at the back of the Atob onto the spotless paved square of Pride. He didn't take any notice of Toity's list of useful facts about accommodation and eating places and banks and museums and Centres of Self Esteem, and other such things that belonged to Pride. Once he had seen the wonderful fountain, there was no room for anything else. He approached the sparkling water. Signs proclaimed it to be miraculous, rejuvenating, self-enhancing, self-revealing, youth-promoting, visionary, mystical, and many other things besides. It was bubbling up from a golden bowl, inside of which played golden statues of mystical creatures and happy humans and odd mixtures of both. Water was springing and dancing from thousands of silver taps. Sprays of water made fantastic patterns and danced in time to haunting music. It was dazzlingly beautiful.

It was the perfect blend of water from the Rivers Self and Mee;

it was essential drinking for all those who wished to be more fully immersed in Pride; it was impossible to resist.

Charlie took a cup from one of the stacks which were available.

Slowly, he reached out to the fountain.

CHAPTER 18
THE FOUNTAIN OF PRIDE

To their surprise, Hugo, Josie, and Ben were not pursued. Henrietta's sacrifice, and the identical rucksack she carried, had, for now, satisfied the border guards of Pride that they had captured their quarry – along with the dangerous foreign substance being smuggled into their territory.

Grimly, the three remaining members of Operation Grey continued threading their way through the trees, until the foliage began to thin. Oddly, it began to change colour too. Dense, dark evergreens gave way to trees of broadleaf varieties bedecked in different colours – until there was nothing but bright, gaudy trees around them. The trees now wore all the colours of the rainbow; none of them had ever seen anything like it before.

The trees thinned until the teenagers found themselves in a manicured park, where neat attendants scanned the plants and trees for any stray leaf out of place. Ben picked a handful of bright red leaves from the low branch of a tree and threw them on the ground. "Give them something to do!" he said gruffly. He now had an intense dislike of Pride.

"It looks ridiculous! Imagine wasting money on this!" said Josie scornfully. She had stopped crying over Henrietta's capture, but she, too, hated Pride for what it had done.

Hugo was trying not to think about his sister. He had taken charge of the Mission Detector and was scanning it. They must focus on finding Charlie. "There's another signal!" he said. "It's flickering… on and off… but it looks like he's approaching the city centre fountain…"

"What fountain?" asked Ben.

Hugo shrugged. "It's gone again," he said, frowning at the small screen. They had been delighted to find that somehow (they weren't sure how) Charlie was emitting a signal. But it was feeble and fading. They must catch up with him before they lost it altogether.

"Ask the Detector where the fountain is!" urged Josie.

"Where is the fountain in Pride?" Hugo asked the Detector.

"Searching for answers," the clipped, mechanical voice of the machine said. After a momentary pause it continued, "Fountain of Pride located in centre of Pride; east-north-east of current location; eleven minutes walk through housing estate; water of fountain dangerous mix of Rivers Self and Mee; must not be imbibed under any circumstances; results of drinking water include: dangerous illusions about self…"

"Quickly!" Hugo lengthened his stride and they all jogged across the park to the only exit they could see. "If Charlie drinks that water, you can imagine what it will do to him in his current state! It will probably undo everything we've tried to do on this journey, and even Henry's sacrifice…!"

They tried to avoid suspicion as they hurried through the streets; but they could not help but be conspicuous – on account of not being accompanied by a Vanitor.

"Where's your Vanitor, dear?" enquired an old lady who was sweeping the spotless pavement outside her immaculate house. "You shouldn't need to carry great big rucksacks like that!"

"We knocked its head off!" said Ben grumpily. He was fed up with Pride and everything that pertained to it. His friend, Charlie, might at this very moment be…

"Ben!" hissed Josie. The old lady was staring at them with interest, and with suspicion too; she *knew* something wasn't quite right. This was no way to proceed through a city which at any moment might be alerted to hunt for a group of teenagers, one of whom carried a large, dark rucksack. What if the old lady reported them to the officials?

"As much as I'm glad the Vanitor *did* lose its head, we probably shouldn't boast about it here," Hugo remarked drily.

"No, sorry," agreed Ben. "I'll think of another excuse. I wonder if they're gullible enough to believe we're evolved Vanitors from another planet…"

"They might believe it, but I'm not sure it's helpful to convince them of that," said Josie.

"After this street of houses we should be able to see the fountain. Not far…" Hugo was scrutinising the map on the Mission Detector. Then he slipped it into his pocket again.

They were approaching a smart-suited businessman, who was walking at a leisurely pace into the city accompanied by no less than three Personal Vanitors. One carried his briefcase, one carried his umbrella, and the third carried a placard which read, '*All-Your-Needs Vanitors Ltd*'. "Where's your Vanitor?" asked the man.

"We're visitors," said Hugo affably, before Ben could invent a more colourful excuse.

"I can recommend my company where you'll get the latest models," said the man, naturally assuming they would be purchasing one. "We manufacture Vanitors for personal and commercial uses, and even develop bespoke models as necessary, although these *do* cost…" He eyed their appearance; clearly he doubted they could afford his prices. Then he snapped his fingers at one of the trailing Vanitors. "Card!" he commanded.

The small robot reached into the briefcase and removed a business card. "We hope to see you soon," it intoned in its cold, mechanical voice.

"Oh, thanks," said Hugo, rather taken aback. He put the card of *All-Your-Needs Vanitors Ltd* in his pocket. "Ow!" He removed it hastily and stuffed it in another pocket while the businessman stared in surprise – and then suspicion.

They hurried away. "What was that about?" asked Josie, when they were safely out of earshot.

"My gold prayer card," said Hugo. "I put the business card in the pocket with the golden card, and…" He removed the business card from his other pocket and they examined it. Not one word remained legible on the card. The company logo, the man's name, the picture of a Vanitor – were all burnt away!

"The golden card doesn't like the idea of Vanitors much!" exclaimed Ben. "Mine blew a Vanitor's head off, and yours has burnt all the details away!"

"Amazing!" said Josie.

They dashed down the street, past the remaining houses. Instinct was warning them to hurry – hurry on to the fountain, even if, in their haste, they attracted attention. And they did attract attention. Too late they realised that a group of black-clothed officials, accompanied by Vanitors, were following them. They turned the final corner and ahead of them was the sparkling fountain, the centrepiece of Pride. Water cascaded in intricate patterns, sparkling and glistening like

172 The Rumour Mill

thousands of diamonds.

"It *is* beautiful," admitted Josie. The gold, the silver, the water glistening like precious stones – it was impossible to deny its splendour.

"Hugo, I don't like to mention the guards, but…" Ben glanced over his shoulder. They were gaining on the Aletheians. Where had they all come from so quickly?

Hugo focussed only ahead. "Charlie first, then we'll worry about the guards."

In the distance, they discerned dozens of people gathered at the fountain. But standing out with crystal clarity was the distinct figure of Charlie. An Atob was driving away, and Charlie had reached the fountain. His hand was stretched out to the water.

The border guards were closing in.

They were too far away, too late to help.

Several things happened at once.

Charlie stretched out his drinking cup towards the fountain of Pride.

Frantically, Ben began to sprint to his friend, shouting his name.

Hugo reached into his pocket for his gold card – and with a desperate prayer for help, threw it the impossibly long distance to the sparkling fountain.

Never, in the entire history of that false and deadly city, had there been such a scene in the centre of Pride. The small, light, golden card could not possibly hope to reach the distance to where Charlie stood at the fountain of Pride. But it took on power of its own, and sped like a guided missile, straight into the heart of the fountain.

WHOOSH!

A great column of water shot straight up into the air! It rose higher and higher for several seconds, not starting to fall until it was far above Pride.

CRACK!

The giant golden bowl which contained the fountain made an awful splintering sound which reached even the outskirts of the city. The silver taps and pipes split in pieces, sending water showering in every direction.

Then the water which was rising into the sky began to fall. It was the most torrential deluge Pride could ever boast of. Atobs and Vanitors went tumbling down the streets and panic-stricken people scrambled for cover. It did not take long for the square around the fountain to become a swimming pool. And Vanitors hadn't been programmed to swim.

But perhaps the most uncanny thing of all was that the water changed. The impact of the golden card of prayer on the waters of Self and Mee was at once tremendous and awful to see. From sparkling and glorious, it became muddy and confused. It was cloudy, dingy, grey, and unpalatable. It contained small wriggling worms and other creatures associated with dirty and dead things. It became, in short, the most disgusting flood the pristine city of Pride had ever had the misfortune to suffer.

In amazement, Hugo and Josie stood and stared at the demolition of the centrepiece of Pride. But they could not linger. There would be dire consequences, and the trained guards of Pride, flabbergasted at the destruction, had not lost sight of *them*.

Josie made a courageous decision. "I must do this, Hugo," she said.

Hugo nodded. He swallowed hard. "I know, Jo."

She handed him a neat bag from inside her rucksack, ready for such an eventuality. It contained all the things she thought might be helpful to continue with the mission.

"Remember you still have your gold card!"

Josie remembered the words etched on the beautiful card which was her prayer token. '*Be anxious for nothing, but in everything by prayer…*'[9] "I won't forget," she said.

The officials of Pride were approaching.

"For the sake of the Truth, and for Charlie's sake," whispered Josie.

And then she turned and walked towards the guards.

CHAPTER 19
HUMBIE HOUSE

Miserably, but without hesitation, Hugo sprinted away from Josie and towards Ben and Charlie. Soon he was wading in foul water, then he was up to his neck, then he was swimming as hard as he could. But something was keeping him afloat, and… was it also propelling him along? The rucksack on his back, with its precious, powerful contents, could not be overwhelmed by the flood around them. And his armour of God[3] would not be deluged by this evil tide. He glimpsed Ben, also easily staying afloat under the protection of his own armour of God. Ben had an arm around Charlie, struggling to tow his friend away from the havoc around them. Hugo pushed aside pieces of 'drowned' Vanitors, and bits of the golden statues from the devastated fountain (which proved not to be gold after all, but light plastic), and other things that were now floating and bobbing in the water. He reached Ben and grabbed Charlie's other arm.

"Jo?" panted Ben.

"Gone," said Hugo grimly.

Ben didn't say anything more. There was nothing to say. This was for Charlie. They had all agreed.

They were not followed by the outraged officials of Err: Josie's sacrifice had seen to that. They reached shallower water which was soaking into parklands on the far side of the fountain.

"Whatz happened?" asked Charlie.

In a wonderful understatement, Ben replied, "They've got a problem in Pride. We need to get out of here!"

Charlie didn't argue. Soaked and weary, with Hugo and Ben occasionally looking over their shoulders to check for pursuers, they moved as quickly as they could through the continuing torrential rain which fell from the broken fountain that still spewed high into the sky. Hugo checked directions on the small Mission Detector – which had suffered no harm from the flood.

"We need to bear further west for Humbie House," he said.

Ben tugged on Charlie's arm.

"Humbie Houze?" echoed Charlie. "I'z heard of zat!"

Hugo was surprised but didn't know whether to believe him. "Have you?"

"Toity, zee tour-guide zaid…" Charlie talked about what Toity had said, and Hugo and Ben, who could make no sense of it whatsoever, said nothing. They were only glad Charlie was compliant and cooperating with them.

The closer they walked towards Humbie House, the more the crowds, which had been rushing away from the devastation at the fountain, dwindled, until they were once more conspicuous – the only three people in the whole of Pride who were going to the only safe place.

The gaudy, rainbow-coloured trees were losing their colour under the unrelenting water; the colours were oozing and sticky and mixing together to create tones of revolting brown mud. Then they thinned out altogether until there were green trees about them. Real daffodils grew in the agreeable parklands, and there was suddenly only light rain – a harmless spring shower. There was recent evidence of tree planting – the types of trees that Hugo and Ben had run through earlier when they escaped from Ms Hauteur and the border guards. But someone had been digging them up.

At last, sticky, soaked, and exhausted, they saw the turrets of Humbie House. The closer they got to the house, the more curious it appeared. It was a large, sturdy house – built to last, with all the money poured into useful things like foundations and thick walls. Pride built its houses to look good on the outside, but Humbie House was built of rough-hewn stone and massive timbers, with no attempt at smooth finishing or ornamentation. But most noticeable of all were the mirrors! The high walls, which enclosed the house, were all made of mirrored-glass. It was a strange place to approach: like walking into the reflected landscape, with someone else walking back towards you.

"Not more mirrors!" exclaimed Ben, thinking of the Vanitors.

But these mirrors weren't like the reflections cast by a Vanitor of Pride.

"They're the mirrors of *Real-Me*," said Hugo, reading from the Mission Detector. "This is definitely Humbie House, it says here…"

They were close enough to the mirrors to see their reflections.

For the first time, Charlie came face to face with the truth of what he was truly like.

He gave a loud cry and fell to the ground.

A large, scruffy, fresh-faced man burst through the mirrored gates of Humbie House. He was dressed in gardening clothes, with dirt under his fingernails and the scent of outdoors about him. Without any hesitation, he hurried to the three bewildered boys. He didn't remark on their soaked and muddy appearance. He got straight to the point.

"Alright, son, let's give you a hand here…" He lifted Charlie in his strong arms. "Right, follow me!"

Ben muttered, "Hugo, are you sure this man's alright…?"

There was definitely nothing of the false façade of Pride about the man, and Hugo said, "Um, are you Outpost Rescuer, Mr Meek, sir?"

"Indeed! Of course!… Didn't have time to… introduce myself… did I? Fisher… Meek…!" Charlie was a tall boy, and Mr Meek panted under the weight of him. "We'll explain everything when… we're safely… indoors… GLADLY…!" The last word was a cry to another occupant of the house. "Gladly! They've arrived!" He deposited Charlie on a large sofa in the hallway – fondly scolding two dogs who had been sleeping there. Nearly squashed by Charlie, the dogs leapt from the sofa and scampered happily from the room, as if they were on a grand adventure. Mr Meek chuckled as he watched them go. "Don't tell Mrs Mcek that Mild and Meekie were on the sofa again," he mumbled to the boys.

The hallway was the size of a large room. It was plain and unpretentious: stone-flagged, wood-panelled, all made of good natural materials. A bright fire was crackling in the hearth. Mr Fisher Meek removed his wellington boots – along with a good sprinkling of soil – and rubbed his grimy hands down his overalls. "Didn't have time to wash up!" he said. "I was digging up those Prideful trees all morning – until the rain came on! The town *will* keep planting them – trying to hide the mirrors of Real-Me, you see? …GLAD!"

A woman came quietly into view. "I heard you the first time, Fisher," she remarked amiably. Her voice was soft and her movements calm, and she went straight to the prone, feebly stirring form of Charlie. "This boy needs help…"

"We know that, Glad," said Fisher Meek good-naturedly. "Quite an adventure you boys have had!"

"Oh, did you know we were coming, sir?" Hugo asked, trying to put together the pieces of this bewildering puzzle.

Mr Meek added another log to the fire. "Been on the lookout for you for hours," he said. "Lieutenant Faithful – what a capable young man he is! – alerted us via our Mission Detector that you were in the city. He had great faith in your ability to make your way here. One girl missing, he said. But where's the other one?"

"Josie – she's gone too," said Hugo.

"They took her?" asked Gladly Meek, aghast. She was bent over Charlie, spooning liquid into his mouth.

Hugo nodded wearily. "She sacrificed herself so we could get away, like my sister did."

Mrs Meek was shaking her head. "Oh my! Those poor girls, poor things…"

"Now, now, Glad," said Fisher. "Don't start to frighten the boys with tales of the guards and inspectors of Pride!"

"And they carried prayer cards," added Ben.

Both Fisher and Gladly Meek brightened. "Gold cards? From the Prayer Academy?" they asked eagerly, talking over the top of each other.

Ben nodded.

Fisher clapped his hands. "Was that what you used at the fountain, boys?" he asked.

"It was my card," said Hugo, surprised at the fame of the golden cards.

Fisher laughed. "I *knew* it was only united, specific prayer that could do that!" he said. "Haven't seen anything on that scale around here for years! When that fountain hit the sky…!"

Suddenly, Charlie sat up. "Greyz!" he said. "I looked greyz in zee mirrorz! Why didn't youz tell me I'z greyz?" And then his pale face looked even more aghast. "Why am I'z zpeaking like ziz?" he asked, terrified. "What haz happened to mez?!"

Fisher Meek approached the couch which Charlie appeared likely to bolt from at any moment. "Now, now," he said comfortingly, "remember, there's nothing about you that the Lord Jesus can't cleanse and put right, son.[5] It's just that you've seen yourself as you truly are in the mirrors of Real-Me. Which can be quite a shock when you've thought you're alright, you see? Quite a wakeup call, I'd say!"

"Butz what iz it? Why am Iz greyz?!"

"Well, I'm not sure I rightly know the whole story behind that, although I would suppose a whole lot of ugly *meddling* has been going on," remarked Fisher.

Ben approached his friend. "It was the Meddlers, Charlie," he said. "The White-Jacket Meddlers, remember? You found them underground…"

"White-Jackets, was it?" muttered Mr Meek, clearly interested in the details. "Thoroughly nasty and dangerous blighters!"

Slowly, some of the confusion cleared from Charlie's face. "I remember zeeing them…" he said. "Butz why…?"

It was a good question, of course. If Charlie's mind was at least clear enough to understand his predicament, there was plenty of explaining to do – not least why they were where they were – in Humbie House, on the outskirts of Pride.

"I'm afraid you're infected, Charlie," said Hugo. "You imbibed the White-Jacket Meddlers' poison, which has turned you grey, and until now has been clouding your mind…"

"Dear me!" exclaimed Mr Meek, putting yet another log on the already blazing fire. "I've never heard of that before, I must say!"

Charlie suddenly got up from the couch. "Iz zat why we'z on ziz journey?" he asked. "Iz it to do wiz zee Meddlerz?"

Neither Hugo nor Ben had any idea how much Charlie was capable of understanding about their mission, or, indeed, how much he *ought* to know about the journey.

"I expect it will all become clear after a good night's sleep," said Mr Meek, detecting the hesitation of the boys. "We'll all have a good chat about it in the morning. And just you remember, young man, that there is a complete cure for whatever has happened to you – there's no defilement that the Lord Jesus can't clean away!"

Charlie's eyes were clear of the grey-cloud which had befuddled him for so long. But the rest of him was as grey as ever. He looked between Hugo and Ben and at hearty, wholesome Mr Meek too. Ben and Hugo seemed anxious, nervous even, as if they weren't sure whether they could trust him. Charlie didn't ask any more questions. He turned to the fire and pretended to watch it; in silence, he ate the delicious tea that the Meeks provided; they took it in turns to have a hot bath in a massive bathtub; then they were shown to their room in the comfortable, unpretentious surroundings of Humbie House.

All the time, Charlie's mind turned and turned as with greater and greater clarity he began to think and remember.

The three boys were given a large dormitory on one of the upper floors of the house. Hugo and Ben spent a while at the window, watching the city of Pride still being watered with the foul fountain which continued to spew high into the sky. Mr Meek predicted that one of the many sinkholes that Pride was plagued with would open up and swallow the fountain entirely. Pride, he said, would always fall. The boys wished they could witness that event.

Charlie ignored the scene at the window and pretended to go to sleep. Eventually, the other two followed suit, exhausted by their long, adventurous day. As soon as he heard their deep, peaceful breathing, Charlie got out of bed. He picked up his torch and crossed the large room to Hugo's rucksack. He carried it to his own corner and examined it in the light of his torch. Inside were a few bits and pieces – a Mission Detector; a couple of chocolate bars; camping equipment; a few spare clothes; a see-through bag with a few belongings in it. Quietly, he emptied the see-through bag. Among the contents that spilled out of the bag was a diary. It was the diary Josie Faithful had kept about their journey – and, in particular, about Charlie Steady.

Charlie began to read. Josie's writing was neat and clear. His disturbed, newly-awakened mind began to grasp the details of the perilous mission upon which they had embarked. He understood, for the first time, the great sacrifice Henrietta had made on his account, and he wondered if Josie, too, had been taken because of him. Was that why he could now read her diary? It seemed that they all thought that somewhere on that journey Charlie might come face to face with his need of cleansing from the Meddlers' poison. Well, they had got *that* right! He now knew how badly he was infected. He had scrubbed at the awful grey coating in the bath: but it made no difference whatsoever. It was engrained in him, part of his very skin.

Josie mentioned love a lot too, but, as Charlie saw it, there was no hope of love and forgiveness for him; there was no way God could overlook everything he had done against Aletheia, against the Truth, *against God Himself*. He had sided with the Meddlers; he had become like them. There was no one to breach the awful chasm he had forged between himself and God.

He picked up the last thing in the rucksack – a large bundle which took up the bulk of the space. It was wrapped in soft cloth and tied with fine string, but it wasn't hard to undo the knot and get into the parcel. He knew what it was. It was mentioned in Josie's diary. It was a prayer token, forged in love, apparently made just for him. *They* thought it would help; *he* thought that nothing could. In bitter anger and despair he took it into his hands and tore it apart.

It disintegrated quite easily in his fingers. It was proof, he thought, of how useless it really was. There was nothing to help the likes of him. He left the shreds of the ruined covering on the floor. Neither of the other boys stirred.

He must go. There was an invisible force compelling him to leave. He was clear-headed enough to know that this was the effect of the poison within him. He was being drawn to the Meddlers – but might he not attempt to destroy these Meddlers who had destroyed him? He knew that he could not stop the poison, nor could he undo what he had done, but at least in this way he might be able to make some sort of amends before he was overcome completely.

There was nothing else to do.

In his despair he could see no hope.

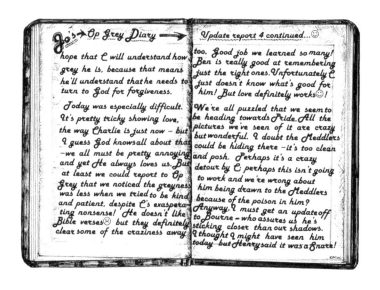

PART 3: THE RUMOUR MILL

CHAPTER 20
BREAKTHROUGH!

Dusty and Flair bent over the Weather Guide machine in the Central Control Room of the Academy of Soldiers-of-the-Cross. They were tense and silent. Nearly everyone in the Control Room had gone home. It was hurrying past teatime and on into the evening, but Mr Brian Buffer, the manager, remained in his cluttered office. There was plenty of paperwork to keep him busy, but he was more interested in watching the two eager students by the Weather Guide. He had, through necessity, become increasingly initiated into the secret of what Dusty and Flair were trying to achieve through their various drastic experiments in the Control Room. Once he understood, he bore with the results of their investigations, even while he doubted they would succeed. But now they were actually on the verge of an interesting breakthrough; he could feel it in his scientific bones.

Recently, Dusty and Flair had been experimenting with the poisonous White-Jacket Meddler vapour which Dr Pentone had managed to reproduce. In their excitement, Dusty had managed to poison Flair who spent a couple of hours in the hospital wing of the Academy. But, despite setbacks, the students remained enthusiastic. Not once had they given up on their experiments – even if no one else thought they would succeed; not once had they considered giving up on their quest to find a link between weather patterns and the location of White-Jacket Meddlers – and from there find the location of the Rumour Mill. It was their own way of helping Charlie. If they could discover the whereabouts of the Rumour Mill, the forces of Aletheia could destroy it. Then Charlie might be freed from the muddle of the Meddlers' poison.

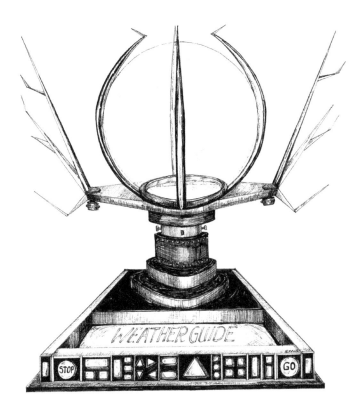

In the clear glass globe of the Weather Guide, angry clouds were gathering. They were all shades of grey, and they were spewing out dirty-white vapour which sizzled and crackled as it hit the sides of the globe – like vicious sparks of lightning. Dusty and Flair were avidly watching the screen below the Weather Guide. This was where detailed information appeared about all sorts of things connected with the weather – patterns, and predictions, and records, for the entire land of Err. You could ask the machine specific questions, you could investigate anything you wanted to about the weather. Just about the only thing you *couldn't* do was make the weather happen.

Suddenly Dusty was speeding away from the Weather Guide to the Storm Tracker device. This device was linked to the information produced by the Weather Guide: but what the Storm Tracker specialised in was *storms*.

Brian Buffer got up from his desk and looked through the window of his office. The large Storm Indicator Glass of the Tracker began to fill with vivid red clouds which tossed and rolled, twisting and turning. But the most curious thing about the red storm clouds was the sinister dirty-white vapour which threaded through and around them like a venomous snake. Mr Buffer gave an inarticulate exclamation and hurried onto the floor of the Control Room.

"I think we've found something, sir!" exclaimed Dusty in excitement.

The manager peered at the small tubes beneath the massive Indicator Glass on the Storm Tracker. One of them was showing an identical storm to the one in the large glass. This indicated which region the storm would hit. "Region seven," he mumbled.

"That's exactly where they are, sir! That's the Region which contains Pride! It *must* be to do with the Rumour Mill!" Flair was too excited to hold back, even though Brian Buffer knew all of this very well.

Dusty, too, was too excited to keep silent. "A red storm, sir! Second highest category! It's going to be a big storm!"

"Bigger than you might imagine." Mr Buffer was thinking hard. He made his way to the Weather Guide, shadowed closely by Dusty and Flair.

"Why is the storm brewing?" asked Flair. Whilst the cleverness of the two students could not be doubted, neither of them knew enough to understand why there might be a *red* storm in connection with the Meddlers and the Rumour Mill.

Dusty added, "Of course, we know the Rumour Mill is a big deal, but why the storm now? Wouldn't the land of Err want to keep the Rumour Mill secret and protect it, and *not* create storms around it?"

"A good question," said the manager. His fingers were flying across the controls of the Weather Guide, pressing a combination of buttons, and flicking switches, and twiddling knobs. Dusty watched admiringly. He wished he knew as much as Mr Buffer did about the marvellous machines in the Control Room. One day…

"I believe the storm is unexpected by the Meddlers. It may be brewing because of Operation Grey and the presence of that poor lad." He meant Charlie Steady, of course. "The area around the so-called Rumour Mill will be thick with the poison and pollution of the lies and slanders of the Meddlers. But if you take into that evil atmosphere the presence of the Truth – such as your team members carry with them, well, there is a clash. And if you think about the lad Steady in particular – who is confused and torn between the Truth and the Meddlers – it's no wonder that a storm is rising. There's a big conflict between the Truth and lies, you see?" He finished pressing buttons and scrutinised the screen.

As they watched, the screen of the Weather Guide changed from the information Flair and Dusty had extracted, which was, '*Storm brewing: location Pride-Resentment*', to:

'*Storm: Category Red; Timescale: 6-12 hours; Exact centre of location: 17.2 miles north-north-east of Pride, in south-south-east forest of Resentment; Storm diameter: 20.1 miles…*'

"Awesome!" exclaimed Dusty.

Suddenly, the manager was all action. "We must alert Captain

Steadfast!" He hurried to the special golden tube which was the direct link to Captain Steadfast and others in high command.

"Did we do it, sir?" asked Dusty anxiously. "Did we find it?!"

Brian Buffer looked back at the two eager students who had worked so tirelessly for this moment. "I think that you might actually have discovered the location of the Rumour Mill!" he said.

CHAPTER 21
BOUND TOGETHER

Ben awoke with a start. It was quiet in Humbie House. The big, solid house slumbered peacefully, despite the gale which had blown up in the night. It rattled at the old windows and gusted down the many chimneys. Was that what had woken him? But then there was the slightest sound from far below in the house. Ben got out of bed and went to the window. The night was dark. The moon of earlier had hidden behind dense, fierce-looking clouds; they were faintly tinged with an angry red and seemed unnatural and sinister. The wind swept through the trees, bending and contorting them as it willed.

Ben turned back and stumbled over Hugo's rucksack. What was it doing close to Charlie's bed? He retrieved his Bible and used its light to see. Dismayed, he found the remains of the precious blanket which had been so painstakingly woven on the Intercessory Machine. It was in tatters. Threads of unspeakable value were strewn uselessly across the floor. Ben picked up a handful of strands. Then he noticed Charlie's empty bed.

"No!" He bounded across the room and began pulling on clothes as fast as he could.

"Ben?" Hugo, though sleepy, was suddenly alert.

"Charlie's gone!"

Hugo, too, leapt from bed and began to fumble for his clothes. He quickly took stock of the bedroom: of Charlie's rumpled, empty bed; of the rucksack; of the ruined, powerful prayer token of Aletheia. The burden he had personally safeguarded this far, that Henry and Josie had been taken captive for, had been destroyed by the very one it was designed to help.

"I'll go for Mr Meek, and alert Bourne," said Hugo. "You run after Charlie – I'll catch up with you in a minute... your armour, Ben! Put on *all* your armour of God..."[3]

In his haste to leave, Ben had almost forgotten about his protective armour. He was a newer Christian than the others; he hadn't been used to putting it on as they had. He strapped the pieces in place. One wave at Hugo, and he dashed for the door.

The two dogs, Mild and Meekie, were once more occupying the sofa in the hallway. They thumped their tails as Ben ran out of the house. Was it them that had alerted him?

"Charlie! Charlie, wait!" Ben could see the figure of his friend moving rapidly ahead.

Charlie was going in the direction of the unfriendly wind, being blown swiftly away from Pride, in the direction of the dire town of

Resentment. At least the wind carried Ben's voice to his friend. Charlie stopped briefly and then, as if he had no will of his own, he began to move on again. Ben ran after him as fast as he could. Whether it was the strange wind, or the power of prayer, which propelled him along, he didn't know. Far quicker than it seemed possible, he reached Charlie and he grabbed him.

"Stop! It's not safe, Charlie! You can't go on alone! Don't you see?"

"Zee?" echoed Charlie, choking back a sob. "Of courze I zee! I'z all wrong! Greyz! Zee Meddlerz haz got me…!"

"But the Lord Jesus can make you right!" cried Ben. "That's what He did for me! He's the only One[18] Who can make you clean and take away the poison of all the lies!"

There were tears on Charlie's cheeks; his eyes were wild and desperate. "Iz lozt," he said brokenly. "Juzt leave me, Benz. Iz got to do one lazt zing right. Zen zey can deztroy it!"

"Do? Do what? Destroy it…?!"

"I knowz all about zee Rumour Millz," said Charlie sadly. "I read Jozie'z diary. It'z me who haz to findz itz…"

"No! It's not like that at all!"

But Charlie wasn't listening. "Juzt leave mez," he said miserably.

"I can't!" said Ben, tightening his hold around his friend, using both his hands to hang on. "We promised, you see? We'll never let you go, and we'll never give up on you!"

"Why can't youz let mez go?!" Charlie tugged violently away from Ben, and Ben clung on with all his strength.

"We can't let you go because we need to keep showing you the love of God!" cried Ben desperately. "It's why Henry and Jo were taken captive! To help you understand how much God loves you! You have to understand…!"

"God can't love mez nowz!"

Ben shook his head, willing Charlie to believe him. "But He does!" he said. "God doesn't love us because we're *lovable*, He loves us *despite* how *unlovable* we are!"

"I'z az bad az zee Meddlerz! Letz go!"

That was the one thing Ben was determined not to do. He had a feeling that if he let Charlie go, the unnatural wind would carry him away. There was an eerie, unnerving quality about this storm with the glittering red tinge which could be seen even through the darkness of night; and there was something horribly familiar about the dirty-white tendrils which were snaking and slithering their way through the clouds, and beginning to gather increasingly around the two boys.

Charlie didn't seem to notice the white vapour, but Ben had spotted it the moment it had begun to sweep around his friend's head. They were outside the secure boundaries of Humbie House; there was nothing to protect Charlie here. Charlie's clear eyes again began to cloud with grey, and, as that happened, he lashed out at Ben. He swung his fist and smashed it onto Ben's nose. Blood began to trickle down Ben's face. But still he didn't let go. Not when Charlie hit him the second time, or the third...

There was a shout, carried on the wind which was rapidly increasing in strength. Fisher Meek and Hugo were coming after them.

Charlie yelled to get away.

Without any warning, lightning-quick, a gust of wind swept Charlie and Ben up in its arms, straight into the heart of the raging red clouds.

Ben heard the startled shouts of Hugo and Mr Meek.

Then he heard no more.

They were in a forest. It was dense and dark and the trees were so thickly crowded together it was impossible to see any distance at all. There was no clue whether the wood was large or small, flat or steep, and where in the world it was, either. The red storm had caught them up and spewed them out somewhere for its own nefarious purposes; the two of them had fallen through the clustered trees into an unknown place.

Slowly, Ben sat up. He put his hand to his face. It came away covered in blood – and he didn't think that was only from where

Charlie had hit him. Probably tree branches had cut him too. He saw his friend sprawled on the forest floor a short distance away. Charlie was lying face down on the dank ground. He began to stir.

Ben wasn't yet sure he could trust his legs. He crawled the short distance to Charlie. They were sheltered from the horrible red storm; it could barely reach through the dense jungle about them. But the dirty-white tendrils of poison could, and Charlie was at their mercy. They crowded around him as if they were doing a horrible, sarcastic, celebratory dance.

Ben reached into his pocket and withdrew a thin, glittering cord. He hadn't been able to get his hands on it earlier; he had been terrified he would lose hold of Charlie. But he had prepared it for such a moment – even when, in the safety of Aletheia, such a situation was unimaginable. Quickly, Ben added the strands he had collected from the covering that Charlie had ruined. He twisted them as fast and as tightly as he could around his cord from Aletheia, hoping they would hold. Then, before Charlie could gather himself again, Ben tied one end of the unusual rope to his wrist, and the other end to Charlie's wrist – binding them together. He had never tested his homemade cord; it was soft and fine and seemed to be made more of shadow than substance, but he was counting on it holding them together.

Charlie felt the soft cord and shook his hand. He sat up and looked at Ben. He observed their wrists joined with the rope. His eyes cleared, despite the evil cloud which surrounded him.

"I'z got to go to itz," he said despairingly. "I'z not strongz enough, you zee? Zee Meddlerz makez me go to itz."

His face was grimy from the forest floor. There were the traces of tears which left a sad trail on his grim, set features.

"Then I'll come too," said Ben simply.

Charlie shook his head, but he didn't otherwise protest; besides, now he was bound to his friend. Charlie began to move unerringly through the trees, pushed along by the horrible white vapour. Ben went with him. He began to pray.

There was a bitter taste in the night air of the never-ending forest of Resentment. And actually, the forest never did end. It surrounded the dark, embittered town in one ceaseless circle of biting, acid shadow. It was a desperately inconvenient place to walk. There was no path, and as soon as you thought you might make progress, huge trees blocked your way and made you take a different route. Branches and tree limbs hung at exactly the wrong height, and leaves and pine needles were jagged and sticky and tore at your hair and clothes. They left tiny cuts and scratches which oozed white acid and stung horribly.

Charlie was now deathly white and he began to be sick. Every so often, he would vomit grey muck which smelt of death and decay, and then he would struggle on – head hung low, desperate and despairing.

Ben didn't comment. He couldn't think of anything to say about Charlie's predicament: it was obvious to both of them, and words about how awful it was wouldn't help. They were being followed by other creatures of Err too: Snares stalked them, their eyes glittering in the shadow of their faces; but they didn't dare approach the light of Ben's Bible. Stumbles carpeted the forest floor, adding to Charlie's struggles. The only comforting thing Ben could do was quote Bible verses, glad he had been made to learn passages about love. "This is how God showed His love to us: He sent His only Son into the world to give us life through Him. True love is God's love for us, not our love for God. God sent His Son to be the way to take away our sins…"[19] The words sizzled on the bitter air, foreign and unwelcome in this sinister, unhappy place. But the power of the Word of God began to dissipate the evil white vapour. The dirty-white clouds reluctantly swooped away from them, unable to penetrate their minds or even fill the air about them with the stench of death. Charlie stopped being sick.

Then, unexpectedly, the trees cleared and the words died on Ben's lips.

Horrified, they stared at the sight before them.

It was the Rumour Mill.

CHAPTER 22
THE INTERROGATION OF PRIDE

Henrietta wasn't sure how long she had been held in the Quarantine Quality Control facility in the territory of Pride. She wondered if *'quality control'* was merely a polite name for exterminating undesirables; and she was certainly one of those. How easily they had all been fooled into thinking that a journey into Pride was as easy as a walk in the park! They all knew the dangers of the land of Err; under the instruction of the leaders of Operation Grey, they had thoroughly prepared for them. But none of them had imagined that a place as nice and posh as Pride was so horribly rotten and evil at its core.

The white-coated staff of the quarantine facility had mostly left her alone, one of dozens of others milling about the Holding Room. She was initially examined by a Vanitor who was larger than the unfortunate Vernon had been, and who left big bruises on her where it had probed and pressed, trying to find any weakness and room for the values of Pride through her armour of God.[3] Of course, Henrietta knew there was no weakness in the armour. The Vanitors and inspectors and guards of Pride could not even perceive it: you had to believe in the Truth of the Bible to appreciate the protection of God's provision. To her delight, they also failed to see the golden card of the Prayer Academy which remained in her pocket. She hadn't forgotten the effectiveness of Ben's card at the Border Assessment Clinic. But she knew she had far more formidable obstacles to overcome here. There were dozens of Vanitors, and guards, and inspectors, all with an eagle eye on the undesirables they had taken to examine.

They had taken the rest of her belongings. All her safe Aletheian food and Water of Sound Doctrine and other provisions were gone. There was a water machine in the room, but the water was a mixture of the Rivers Self and Mee, and she would not touch it. Valiantly, she had so far managed to ignore her growing thirst and gnawing hunger.

The darkness of night fell beyond the windows. There was a storm brewing. It was strange and red-tinged and angry. Coloured storms in the land of Err always meant something significant; Henrietta wondered if this one was in any way connected to the Rumour Mill and the events which might be transpiring there while she was locked away.

The Holding Room was large and clinical – and see-through. Its walls were made of clear material, so clear that it was common for the people milling around the room to walk into them. There were no beds or blankets or anything conducive to a good night's sleep. Pride didn't stop or sleep; it carried on through night-time much as it did during the day. The workers of Pride worked shifts; the undesirable people in the Holding Room were interrogated whenever the officials of Pride pleased, no matter the time.

Guards and inspectors roamed through the rooms on the other side of the clear walls. The unfortunate people in the Holding Room could see everything that happened there. People were gathered, like animals, for assessment. They could watch them being examined by Vanitors and inspectors on the other side of the invisible barrier.

Watching those found to be inadequate by Pride being examined and treated was an awful but intriguing sight. Henrietta was transfixed when a woman, covered in odd bits of sticking plaster, including on her clothing, was taken in hand by a large Vanitor. An obese inspector oversaw the proceedings. The inspector was a massive woman who had a gold chain about her, like a medal of honour.

She watched as the Vanitor removed all the bandages from the woman. They weren't doing any good anyway so it made no difference – although the woman yelped in pain each time one was removed.

Henrietta knew the woman

with the plasters was from the town of Broken; she had been there and seen the poor people who thought they could cover their brokenness with sticking plasters.[13] But she knew that wasn't the answer. Only the Lord Jesus could heal the brokenness of sin. The poor lady had come to the wrong place!

The woman vanished for a moment with the Vanitor, and reappeared in different clothing – smart, tailored and particular. Then a hairdresser got to work. Then a make-up artist with a significant hoard of supplies came and stationed himself on a stool. He changed the woman's face, plastering over harsh, cracked lines, adding splashes of colour, and painting her lips into a smile. The woman with the pretend smile was then approved for entry.

Again and again, Henrietta watched the deceptive treatments of Pride on folk who needed the Lord Jesus to heal them of their many ailments – all caused by sin. Pride was so full of deceit – everyone was kidding themselves. What lies she saw being practised on people who were treated in the wrong way! How quickly they were soothed by the vain treatments of Pride!

Henrietta knew she would not be so easily 'fixed' by Pride. Soon, perhaps very soon, the city officials would realise that the contents of her rucksack were not what Pride was searching for, despite the fact that the rucksack had been prepared to mislead them. Soon the inspectors of Pride would realise that the foreign substance they had sensed and felt so threatened by was still at large somewhere in their territory. Then the border guards would come for her again. Henrietta fingered the prayer card in her pocket. Should she use it…?

She was contemplating how best to make use of the most powerful weapon she had, when there was a stir in the assessment area on the other side of the screen. A large group of black-clothed guards appeared, swaggering their way into the melee of folk being inspected and treated before being allowed to enter Pride. They thrust a girl before them, making it clear that she was to go to the front of the long queue.

Henrietta gasped.

It was Josie!

Josie was bruised and bleeding. They had been rough enough with Henrietta when she had been taken, but Josie had been captured at the scene of the worst 'terrorist' attack Pride had witnessed in years. And *she* was thought to be the perpetrator! Josie sank to her knees, unable to stand. A brute of a Vanitor Henrietta had not seen before walked robotically into the room with jerky steps. The Vanitor roughly searched Josie, obviously bruising and hurting her as its unforgiving metal claws probed her. It found a small object wrapped in a cloth and handed it to a watching guard. The guard took it cautiously with a gloved hand, immediately putting it into a clear, plastic bag; he handed it to a white-coated inspector who rushed away with it. Henrietta groaned. She couldn't see within the wrappings of that cloth, but she guessed that Josie's precious golden prayer card was now in the grubby, undeserving hands of an inspector of Pride. How like Josie to keep her golden card carefully clean within wrappings!

The Vanitor now reached with brutal metal fingers and grasped Josie round the neck, yanking her to her feet. The people in the Holding Room clustered curiously at the clear screen, crowding around Henrietta. It was obvious to all of them that this girl was a captive of great importance: and she was here for interrogation, *not* for treatment. Questions were being put to the captive, although Henrietta and those with her couldn't hear them. The slightest shake of Josie's head and the massive Vanitor tightened its hold around her neck. She whimpered and began to choke. But still she shook her head at their questions.

Henrietta whispered her cousin's name in horror. Not so long ago, nobody would have thought that vain, selfish Josie Faithful would stand for the Truth with such wonderful courage. Henrietta knew she didn't have time to hesitate. Her precious gold card must be used for Josie's sake – no matter what they might do to her once they understood the two girls were connected and part of the same 'terrorist' gang. In addition, Ms Hauteur might turn up at any moment and inform them of that fact. She must act while she still had the advantage of surprise.

As the crowd of broken, inadequate, undesirable people in the Holding Room pressed around Henrietta, she withdrew the golden card from her pocket and held it in a trembling hand. With a clear, bold voice she cried, "This is the power of Bible Truth!" and she flung it with a desperate prayer at the see-through wall, towards the group surrounding the helpless form of Josie.

CRACK!

There was the most tremendous crash, followed by clouds of dust and debris and awful shouts of dread and dismay.

Henrietta could hardly believe the evidence of her own eyes when the dust began to clear. She was standing on the edge of a crater – on the rim of an enormous chasm. She hadn't heard of the sinkholes of Pride. She knew the verse 'Pride goes before…a fall',[17] but she had no knowledge of the sudden, dreadful sinkholes which swallowed parts of Pride without warning. They were seldom spoken of. Pride covered them up as quickly as they could, pretending they didn't exist at all. But there was no doubt of this: her enemies were gone.

Gone were the Vanitors and guards and inspectors of Pride. Gone, too, was the see-through barrier of the Holding Room. Behind her, the undesirable rejects of Pride still clustered, safe because she stood between them and the destruction. The only other living thing still visible was the girl lying on the brink of the dreadful pit.

It was Josie.

CHAPTER 23
THE FINAL LIE

Ben and Charlie knew that things could not end well. They stood before the horror of the Rumour Mill. One was infected by its poison, struggling even to stand. The other was protected by the armour of God,[3] but too frightened even to pray. Ben had already used his precious golden card; the magnificent prayer blanket, which might have provided protection against the evil they faced, had been ripped to shreds by Charlie in his despair. Now nothing stood between them and their utter destruction by the ghastly, shadowy hordes of Meddlers before them.

They were standing at the edge of a sudden clearing in the dense forest. Immediately before them was a graveyard, ancient and timeless, with ghostly grey headstones casting eerie shadows. Here long-forgotten people of Pride and Resentment lay buried. There was no evidence of the red storm, but there was so much dirty-white vapour here that it appeared as a fine mist, shifting around and between the gravestones. It was a terrifying scene: made of many pieces of nightmares gathered together and spewed out into this one moment.

Above the scene of the buried dead rose the ruin of what was once a grand old house. It had no roof, but its stone walls were standing, like a skeleton without substance; there was no glass in the windows,

212 The Rumour Mill

but all the gaping holes were in place, like dead sockets without the life and sparkle of eyes. Tall chimney stacks were intact and stately, but lifeless too, with only the poison of the Meddlers for smoke.

For a moment the two boys were unnoticed by the silent, ghost-like hordes of Meddlers. For a moment there was silence too. It was clear an unseen barrier was protecting the true sight and sound of what lay ahead. They were standing, as if on the brink of a precipice, before the hideous headquarters of the Meddlers. Charlie hesitated one last time. His head was clear of the muddling lies of the Meddlers through Ben's quoting of Bible verses, and Ben knew he had one final chance to explain the Truth, before Charlie stepped into the precincts of the Rumour Mill and the Meddlers carried him away.

Once more, he began to quote the same verses about God's love. "This is how God showed His love to us: He sent His only Son into the world to give us life through Him. True love is God's love for us..."[19] At that moment, everything Ben had learned about the greatness of God's unconditional love made sense. He must show love to Charlie, even when Charlie had led him to this awful place of death; it was still only a tiny reflection of God's great, unqualified love for him.

"God can't lovez me nowz," said Charlie despondently. But was there at least a question in his tone?

"That's the Meddlers' final lie!" cried Ben. "They'll tell you God doesn't love you, but it's a lie! Because *God is love!*"[20]

At last, *at last*, Ben saw the first glimmer of hope light Charlie's tortured eyes.

He pursued, "Remember the Bible verse? 'God demonstrates His own love towards us, in that *while we were still sinners*, Christ died for us'!"[16]

"While we were ztill zinners," repeated Charlie.

"Exactly! Whatever we've done, God can forgive us. And the death of the Lord Jesus is the proof of God's love."

Charlie stared at Ben's damaged, bleeding face. He had caused that. He looked at the multi-stranded cord which still held them together. Despite what he had done, his friend had still come after him. In a faint but unmistakable way, his friend Ben, and the others, had showed to him the shadow of sacrificial love. At last his mind awoke to the glorious possibility that the love of God didn't depend on him being lovable, but it rested on the determination of an unfailing, unchanging God[21] to show His love to him in the most unmistakable way: through the sending of the Lord Jesus to take away the sin of the world.

Beyond any doubt, Charlie knew he deserved the punishment of God because of his sin; everyone in the world did[22]. God is holy and just and true and must punish sin. But the Lord Jesus came to take the punishment for sin; He bridged the chasm between God and sinful, damaged people. *He* became the mediator[23] Who could reconcile[24] the enemies of God with God Himself. The love of God had stood the ultimate test; it could not fail now.

"It doesn't depend on me at all!" mumbled Charlie. "It all depends on the work of the Lord Jesus, and all I need to do is trust Him! And God will make me right because of Him…"

"Charlie?!" exclaimed Ben. "Charlie! You're speaking right…!"

"I believe God, Ben!" cried Charlie. "If He loved me enough to send the Lord Jesus, then His love is enough for me! I'm trusting in the Lord Jesus! I'm made right!"

Ben gave a cry of triumph. "And you're speaking right! The grey has gone…!"

There was no doubt that Charlie was set free from the poison of the Meddlers. No longer did they have any claim on him. But their enemies were at last alerted to their presence, and before the two boys could flee the scene they were surrounded.

There were Meddlers of every type and colour: clever, vicious, subtle, deceitful, cruel, poisonous – each had their specialty. Charlie and Ben were shoved forward by minuscule jagged fingers, which held tiny, malevolent, needle-sharp swords. That final step forward took them across an invisible line into the horror of the Rumour Mill.

Now they were in the bubble of sound. Like a chorus of hungry crows, the croaks and cries of Meddlers filled the night sky. One moment there had been nothing but silence, and the next, there was the most abominable clamour. It was suddenly clear that there was a strange, protective bubble around the Rumour Mill – and what you could perceive from the outside was nothing to what was really within.

Around and about, overrunning the whole appalling ruin, were tens of thousands, and thousands upon thousands of Meddlers. Now they were inside the Rumour Mill, the Meddlers could be seen more clearly in all their sinewy, ugly detail. And the smell! Perhaps the very worst thing about this awesome scene was the stench of death and decay which was now unleashed. It was as if all the long-dead bodies in the graveyard were no longer sleeping beneath the ground, but were decomposing and stinking under the night sky.

Precisely what the Meddlers were doing in the ruin was not immediately clear, and neither of the boys was clear-sighted and calm enough to take stock of the organised activity taking place there. They struggled valiantly against the tide of tiny bodies which were cutting with their jagged fingers and toes and piercing them with hundreds of needle-sized blades. But neither of the boys was any match for the Meddlers' combined strength.

Quickly, the Meddlers closed ranks around them. They pushed and shoved them roughly across the uneven graveyard. They pulled at their hair and their clothes. They hurled abuse. Some troublemakers threw stones and missiles, although the Meddlers were so closely packed about the boys that they did more harm to their own kind than to Ben and Charlie. The only thing they could not do was break the tie between the two captives. They did not dare to tamper with that cord; it burned their evil touch, and one Red-Jacket Meddler who dared to wrestle with it exploded in a puff of red smoke.

Some semblance of order was created when a Blue-Stocking Meddler, taller and more stately and with far better English than the others, appeared among them. He was a captain and the mass of Meddlers did not dare to ignore him. "Stop, you fools!" he hissed. "Don't take them into the centre of our operations! We'll deal with them here!"

The Captain's cruel, cunning face examined both of the boys. He fluttered before them on tiny cobwebbed wings: an incongruously minute, but utterly formidable foe.

Charlie turned to Ben. His eyes were calm, even happy. He had never thought to be cured of the poison of the Meddlers; he had never thought the love of God was so great that it would reach him when he had gone so far away! His mind was still reeling from its extraordinary healing and cleansing. Wave after wave of remembered Truth washed over him as things which he had learned as a child, and rejected as a teenager, at last became real to him. There was absolute Truth! The Lord Jesus Himself *was* the Truth![18] How could he have believed so many lies? But now, was there even the remotest chance they could escape from this place of death alive? This might be his only chance to show that he trusted God: and so he would trust to the end, no matter what.

Charlie could feel Ben working at the knots he had made in the cord around their two wrists. He wished he knew what Ben was thinking. What was it about that cord…?

The Meddlers howled in fury, their boos and hisses making a horrendous din. Almost the entire Rumour Mill was now aware of them. Thousands of Meddlers were crowding around and closing the sky above them as they descended in numberless hordes. The needle swords were unleashed in many hands; Ben and Charlie were punctured by them again and again.

The cord was free. A few Meddlers realised what had happened, but their cries of alarm were drowned by the motley crew who were crowding in, urged to action by more Meddler leaders who were arriving thick and fast.

AHHHH!

With all his remaining strength, Ben whipped the freed cord around the surrounding circle of jeering Meddlers. With cries of alarm, the fluttering creatures fell back from the burning torment of the cord. The strands sparked and flamed and shone like the brightest star in that dark place. Again and again the rope drove the Meddlers back, and, when Ben was tired, Charlie gladly took his turn.

The Meddlers could not overcome the bright, burning cord, but it was a forlorn hope. The boys could not continue indefinitely; they could not keep the encircling, jeering Meddlers away much longer, and the poisonous white vapour was sapping their energy too.

The Meddlers were edging closer, urged to seize the boys by the brutal Meddler guards. They did not care how many Meddlers were burned and died in the attempt; there were thousands more to replace them. Many Meddlers were cut across the middle by the flying strands. They exploded in clouds of coloured smoke, oozing tinted vapour like blood.

Ben prayed frantically.

Charlie thanked God that, whatever happened, he was forever free from the Meddlers' poison.

Thousands of Meddler swords flashed in the light of the burning cord.

There was only a moment before they would be finally overcome.

CHAPTER 24
INTO THE STORM

Lieutenant Faithful scrutinised the heavily fortified Quarantine Quality Control facility from the cover of the dense, unfriendly trees. He knew from Fisher Meek and Hugo that Josie had also been taken, but rescuing Henrietta and Josie from this evil place was not a mission to take lightly.

Then, through the darkness, as the eerie red storm swooped and swirled over Pride, Bourne and his group of hand-picked Rescuers watched in amazement as a large portion of the stark, ominous quarantine facility crashed into the middle of the most devastating sinkhole. Pride had spent a considerable amount of money ensuring the official buildings of the city didn't fall foul of the hidden problem in the town; they had filled vast areas with concrete to ensure there was something solid underneath their important institutions. There was only one explanation for this disaster: Henrietta or Josie had used the powerful weapon of a golden prayer card to overcome their enemies.

Suddenly, all the barriers between the two girls and their freedom vanished into an ugly abyss. Bourne and his Rescuers wasted no time. They made the most of the chaos in the immediate aftermath of the destruction and rushed for the ruined, half-vanished centre. The rescue of Henrietta and Josie was straightforward, but it was complicated by the number of additional people who also wanted to be rescued. Henrietta's words about the power of Bible Truth, when she used the golden card, had had a far greater impact than she could have anticipated.

While dazed black-clothed officials made frantic calls to the Council of Pride and tried to regroup and arrange lighting to see what was happening in the darkness of the red storm, Rescue Capsules, the fantastic flying machines of the Rescuers, arrived by air from Aletheia. Soon, a dozen relieved, weeping people, who had been with Henrietta in the Holding Room, were on their way back to the city of Truth.

As the Rescue Capsules departed, to her surprise, Henrietta glimpsed the woman from Broken whose sadly ineffective treatment she had observed. How she had become part of the group who were rescued she had no idea, but it was definitely her. The heavy plastering of make-up on the woman's face was streaming under her tears. The painted smile was wonky and smudged, looking as if it was about to fall off her face completely. But she was heading in the right direction. In Aletheia she could be fixed from the inside out; then she could truly smile again.

These poor people, who had been deemed inadequate by the assessment of Pride, would not receive lies as treatment in Aletheia. They would not be re-dressed, and made-up, and groomed, and given painted smiles, and surgically re-aligned, and offered gallons of 'healing' water from the Rivers Self and Mee, and offered weird and wonderful concoctions for mind-alteration, and whatever other fixes they offered in Pride. Instead, they would learn that, despite how awful they truly were, the love of God could reach them and offer full and complete restoration because of the sacrifice of the Lord Jesus when He died on the cross. Aletheia would take the undesirables of Pride and give them far richer treasures!

It was with some misgivings that Lieutenant Bourne Faithful did not dispatch his injured sister, Josie, and his young assistant, Henrietta, straight back to the hospital wing of the Academy of Soldiers-of-the-Cross in Aletheia. But Josie, shocked and injured though she was, was insistent that she needed to go where Charlie was – she had unfinished business there. Henrietta had no idea what Josie, in her current state, could possibly achieve. But she would not doubt her. Bourne, full of admiration for all that both girls had sacrificed and done, could not resist their pleas.

"Ready, Henry?" Bourne gestured to the waiting capsule – Capsule

First-John-Four-Nine, more simply known as First-John. It was a small, neat capsule built for speed, and was the first of a fleet of elite John-Capsules which were continuing on the mission, following the dozens of other Rescue Capsules already dispatched from Aletheia. They were heading to the location discovered by Dusty and Flair. They were going to the Rumour Mill.

There were only five people in the main cabin of Capsule First-John. Henrietta and Josie were two of these; the other three were grim-faced Rescuers. Josie had revived somewhat. She had been drinking the Water of Sound Doctrine, and had applied the soothing ointment of FaintNot – one of Dr Pentone's personal remedies – onto her cuts and bruises. Somewhere along the route of her capture by the guards of Pride, Henrietta had sprained her ankle. She wrapped it in a bandage that Josie had found in the first aid kit. "In case we're needed on the ground," she whispered to Josie. Of course, Bourne had been very clear that they would *not* be needed on the ground. Their part in the action had been heroic, but was now over. But Henrietta figured that she should be prepared, just in case…

Capsule First-John shot unerringly through the darkness, taking no time at all to gain on the fleet of Rescue Capsules speeding from Aletheia for the Rumour Mill. Once Dusty and Flair had pinpointed the whereabouts of the Meddlers' sanctuary, a plan was formed.

When the call came through from Fisher Meek that Ben and Charlie had been taken by the storm, the plan was rapidly put into action. The secret of the mission was over: now all of Err – if they were awake – could see the might of the city of Truth heading to the rescue of the two boys, and to complete the destruction of the evil which was the Rumour Mill.

Capsule First-John overtook the other capsules, and, with Capsules Second-John and Third-John as their companions, flew to the forest of Resentment. Henrietta and Josie gathered from the instructions of Lieutenant Faithful, who was liaising with the other capsules and with the three Rescuers in the main cabin, that their small force was tasked with rescuing Ben and Charlie; the vast force following them would deal with the Rumour Mill. Henrietta wondered what would happen if Charlie still hadn't recognised his need and didn't want to be rescued. Would he be forever lost?

As they approached the forest of Resentment, they began to feel the effects of the red storm which was still in the vicinity of the Rumour Mill. Much of it had blown itself away once Ben and Charlie had been taken by it: the storm had snatched the cause of it – which was the infected, confused Charlie – to itself. But around the Rumour Mill, outside the protective bubble, the wind still raged, and angry red clouds swooped and swirled. Capsule First-John bore the buffetings of the storm splendidly. There were a few stomach-churning moments when it swooped and dived through the winds, but nothing could deter it from reaching its destination.

"Um, coordinates achieved, Lieutenant…" Henrietta and Josie heard the voice of the pilot filling the main cabin of the capsule. But he sounded puzzled.

Immediately, the three Rescuers swivelled their seats and peered out of the capsule's windows, searching through the red-tinged skies to view the impossibly dark and dense forest below. Josie and Henrietta did likewise.

They were hovering above a clearing in the forest, although they weren't quite stationary because the wind continued to buffet them. The forest clearing was a horribly spooky place – a spectral ruin in the middle of a graveyard. White-mist floated like ghosts through the tombs, but the whole place was utterly deserted. There was no sight or sound of anything at all.

"Shall we search elsewhere, Lieutenant?"

"Hold position," ordered Bourne. "Hold, Second and Third," he directed their accompanying capsules.

"There's nothing here," mumbled Henrietta to Josie. Was it all over? Had the headquarters of the Meddlers already relocated because they knew they were discovered? Had they taken Charlie and Ben with them?

To her surprise, one of the so far silent Rescuers, a man called PeaceBe, spoke. He was a massive man and forbidding in appearance, but his name spoke of the peace which all Rescuers sought to bring. "The fact that you can't see them doesn't mean they're not there. They're the masters of trickery and disguise."

Henrietta was intrigued at this insight. "Do you know all about Meddlers?"

"I've fought them many times," returned the Rescuer. He nodded at the fearful ruin below them. "This place is just where they'd be likely to be!"

"Why?"

"Death," said the Rescuer grimly. "See the tombstones? Meddlers love to be near death. I think they thrive on the air of decay."

Henrietta shuddered. Poor Ben and Charlie might, even now, be captive down in that dreadful ruin.

Suddenly, in the stillness, there was a flash of golden light, spinning like a circle again and again. It was wonderfully glorious light for such a dark, evil place.

"It might be Charlie and Ben!" cried Henrietta.

Josie roused herself, pulling her bruised, aching body from her seat to look more closely.

Bourne Faithful abruptly appeared in the main cabin, slipping into a harness, snapping belts and buckles in place. He barked the command, "Prepare for immediate Air Drop. PeaceBe, you're with me." Private PeaceBe immediately strapped himself into his own harness. Within seconds, the two formidable Rescuers were ready.

A hole in the floor of the capsule suddenly opened up. It was a small-ish hole, about the size of a big Rescuer. Bourne winked at the two startled girls, then, without hesitation, he jumped through the hole, immediately followed by PeaceBe. The girls watched them begin to tumble through the air. They were heading for the fight of their lives: for the sake of two hopelessly outnumbered boys they trusted were still alive.

Before the hole in the floor of the Rescue Capsule could close again, Josie suddenly came to life. She was clutching something tightly in her hand – and she flung it straight through the hole in the floor. It was the last remaining golden prayer card. She had hidden it from her captors. She had even wrapped up a chocolate bar to mislead them – which they had taken for analysis. She had protected her prayer card for Charlie – desperately hoping it might yet save him. She was using it for his sake, and for Ben, and for the sake of her brother and PeaceBe too.

The golden card flew like a rocket from the capsule, quickly overtaking the tumbling Rescuers. The two Rescuers deployed golden parachutes and guided them to the shelter of the trees.

But prayer went before them: and the results were wonderful.

CHAPTER 25
THE LAST PRAYER CARD

The carefully woven covering of strands of deceit and slander, with multitudes of threads of white-lies and black-lies and all the lies in between, strengthened by ties of dishonesty and trickery, made invisible by the beads of disguise, and made invincible by the self-deception of pride – all hid the Rumour Mill from the eyes of the outside world, and cushioned the cacophony of discord to silence. But when the last golden prayer card hit that unholy layer, the whole of the Meddlers' protection was utterly destroyed. There was no big explosion. No fireworks. No sound. Only the sudden illumination of the Meddlers' vile works for everyone to see. Their entire operation was suddenly naked and bare and thoroughly exposed by the Truth.

The golden card went on falling until it hit the circle of Meddlers who had taken two boys captive. A shaft of golden light suddenly illuminated the whole scene, driving the Meddlers back – shrieking and stumbling over the gravestones. They held their hands over their eyes; they couldn't see anything through that glorious light; they could no longer torment the two boys who were lying in pain on the ground in the middle of them.

"A golden prayer card!" whispered Ben feebly, staring in awe at the small golden rectangle which was emitting such incredible light.

Charlie, who knew he had a lot to catch up on, didn't know much about the prayer cards except from the references in Josie's diary. And all the members of Operation Grey were, as yet, unaware of the fact that each one had been used on behalf of others and not selfishly – which had yielded far more spectacular results.

Charlie turned his head to view his friend, stricken and bleeding from countless pin-prick wounds. Charlie was badly wounded too, but both boys felt fresh energy from the radiant light of those golden beams. It was enough to escape. Together they crawled slowly and painfully into the thick trees on the outskirts of the Rumour Mill. At every moment they thought they might be stopped and taken captive once more; but the glorious light hid them from view.

Ben sank onto the forest floor. This was as far as they could go.

"Did you see them?" whispered Charlie.

Just beyond the trees, they could see the exposed Rumour Mill – no longer hidden or quiet in the least. The alarmed cries of the Meddlers screeched across the sky, rending the night apart.

"The capsules in the sky?" asked Ben faintly.

"I think the Meddlers' cover is blown!" mumbled Charlie.

Ben managed to croak a laugh. "I bet the prayer card did that too!"

Charlie whispered hopefully, "Perhaps they've come to rescue us."

Ben's voice was faint but encouraging. "Of course they have," he said. "That's the way it works in Aletheia, remember? If you pray, someone is dispatched to rescue you!"

"Indeed, sometimes even before you pray!" To their astonishment, another voice, that of a man, spoke from the dark forest. Lieutenant Bourne Faithful stepped into view from the cover of the trees, followed by Private PeaceBe. "It seems we were hardly needed," remarked Bourne. "I think this battle has been fought for us – with the help of my sister and the support of some remarkable prayer warriors!" He knelt down by the two boys. He examined Ben – bruised and bloodied from wounds too numerous to count. "You fought well, lad," he said gently.

"He saved my life!" whispered Charlie.

"*God* did that," muttered Ben.

"Praise the Lord!" rumbled PeaceBe in his deep voice. He took his stance by the edge of the trees, observing the Meddlers, guarding the boys. "So many," he mumbled to himself. "Thousands upon thousands…" Meddler captains and leaders and guards were doing their best to restore order to their frightened cohorts. The red storm had blown away; it also could not withstand the prayer card. The light from the golden card shone like the sun, exposing the Meddlers' every move. "They're regrouping, sir," said PeaceBe. "They might plan to get away. Permission to get closer…"

"Permission granted. But observation only. No action yet, PeaceBe."

"Yes, sir," PeaceBe grunted in return and vanished, moving silently around the outskirts of the Meddlers' encampment, taking note of everything he saw.

"PeaceBe is the best Meddler hunter and fighter we've got on the force," said Bourne. "He's been in hundreds of fights and knows all their ways. But I doubt he's ever seen anything on this scale before."

Bourne was now scrutinising Charlie. There was no doubt of his salvation – it showed in every part of him which was cleansed of the grey contamination. But there were countless wounds, and both boys were now sinking under the tiny amounts of Meddler poison with which they had been pierced too many times. They lapsed into silence, barely conscious. There was little Bourne could do to treat their many wounds. Surely help was not far away now…

Hugo had not been idle or lonely. Once the report of Ben and Charlie being snatched by the ghastly red storm had been relayed to the proper authorities, Fisher Meek set about preparing for their own journey to the action at the Rumour Mill. Hugo liked Mr Meek. He was a plain man of decisive, courageous action, and he didn't once consider leaving Hugo behind in safety.

Hugo made his own preparations. They didn't take long. In the light of his Bible, he collected strands and patches of the precious blanket which had been woven for Charlie on the Intercessory Machine. Hugo was a poor sewer, and he was glad Henrietta wasn't around to remark on his efforts – although he wished she was there for many other reasons. But at last he had done all he could to piece back together most of the glorious protection they had carried so far. If and when it could be used, he didn't yet know.

Before the night was much older, Fisher Meek had packed everything necessary into his Rescue Craft and they were ready to go. He said a cheerful farewell to his wife, as if he was simply going on a shopping trip for the weekly groceries. She, in turn, asked him to visit the Bittertwixes in Resentment if he got a chance, as if they were going on a family outing. The utter lack of panic was altogether reassuring, but Hugo knew Mr Meek was expecting trouble. His Rescue Craft was packed with emergency supplies.

The first part of the journey was over the parklands and fields which lay between Pride and Resentment. The Rescue Craft made excellent time: it knew all the bumps and potholes to avoid, which increased as they got closer to Resentment. Resentment was not a place to access smoothly or easily.

Mr Meek didn't hesitate when they reached the first of the trees and entered the dark, dense forest of Resentment. Branches hung down at the wrong height, and some lay strewn across the rough road – such as it was. But this was Fisher Meek's territory; he had plenty of experience of dealing with this obstinate terrain. To Hugo's surprise, he had adapted his Rescue Craft so that it could cut branches and lift them out of the way. Several metal arms slid out from the truck and Fisher guided them unerringly to cut and clear the way.

"Everything around Resentment is difficult," he remarked. "It's the nature of the place. The weather is impossible to predict – because it resents being told what might happen and will do the opposite! The carrots resent being told they're carrots, so they try and grow into potatoes. You can imagine what poor diet the town has! Of course, the people are bitter about everything possible. The whole town is, as you might expect, seething with resentment. Everyone belongs to a society or charity or committee which has been set up to foster their own brand of bitterness and resentment. There's the *Society of Sensitive Souls*, all sorts of committees for scrutinising past grievances, there are *inward-looking* societies that concentrate on *self-issues*, *outward-looking* societies for apportioning blame, there's even the *Society of*

Wrongly-Smacked Children! You name it, the people of Resentment have given it a label and promote it as a worthy cause to be bitter about! It's uphill work here. It's hard to teach people the Truth of God's love and how it can reach them despite their bitterness when they are so set on nursing past grievances!" He sighed as he skilfully manoeuvred the metal arms of the Rescue Craft to lift a particularly large branch out of the way.

They heard the noise of the Meddlers long before they reached the two injured boys. A cacophony of harsh cries and croaks and screeches filled the night. Deeper and deeper they went into the forest, travelling with no obvious path to guide them. Mr Meek followed the Mission Detector advice, and although his face was grim, he never showed any sign of reluctance or fear at what they might face ahead.

At last, when it seemed the awful noise could not possibly grow louder, with the stench of death in the air, and poisonous white-vapour seeking any weakness in them, they encountered the resolute figure of Bourne Faithful in the forest ahead, standing directly in their pathway, watching their approach on his own Mission Detector.

There was no time for small talk, no time for anything but rescue.

"In here," said Bourne tersely.

Mr Meek and Hugo hurried under the branches of trees to the very edge of the Rumour Mill itself. Lying on the forest floor were Ben and Charlie.

Mr Meek and Hugo quickly loaded Charlie and Ben onto the two sturdy beds inside the large Rescue Craft. The boys were as cosy with pillows and blankets as any bed they had ever slept in. But that did nothing for their many wounds. They had been pierced with the sharp needle-swords of the Meddlers too many times. The poison of the Meddlers was in them, and they were now barely conscious.

Mr Meek gave them Water of Sound Doctrine to drink, spooning it patiently into their mouths; then he examined the worst of their injuries in the light of his Bible.

"Sir, if I may…" Hugo bent over the boys. In his hands he held the hastily mended patchwork blanket which had originally been woven on the Intercessory Machine in the Prayer Academy. Strangely enough, it didn't appear so hastily mended now. It seemed other work had taken place besides Hugo's efforts, and the patches which belonged together were once more tightly, skilfully woven.

"A prayer covering?" asked Fisher, his expert eye wandering over the fantastic patterns.

He could detect the intricate, delicate work of patience;

The soft but strong weave of kindness;

The plain, contented portions of no-envy and no-boasting: unadorned but pleased to highlight the lovely patches by which they were surrounded;

The small, discreet, scraps of politeness: pleasantly moulded to give way to other portions;

Selflessness had patches whose strands were so flexible they gave but did not break;

The silky, soothing threads belonged to pieces which allowed no provocation;

No record of wrong was kept by the quietly overlooked pieces which were easily forgotten: they were impenetrable and sturdy and had no pattern at all;

The light, white patches were those of Truth; there was no room for darker stitches;

The thick, multi-stranded patches of strong wool, which bore any wear and tear, completely covered faults and stains from the view of others.

It was a protection that endured; that had been forged even when the one for whom it was intended didn't believe at all. It erred on the side of love, believed the best, hoped for the lost one to come back to God, endured ripping and tearing, and was mended again.

Fisher Meek shook his head in amazement. "Now I know what all the fuss was about in Pride," he said. "Such valuable protection and healing for the error of deceit and pride! There is no room for any of their values here – no wonder the forces of Pride detected and detested it! No wonder they wanted to destroy it – but yes, by all means, quickly, Hugo, this is a cure which nothing else will give; it will treat the wounds and lies and hatred of the Meddlers…"

As Hugo laid the mended blanket over Ben and Charlie, it seemed to him that they stirred in comfort, at last sinking into the peaceful sleep of recovery and relief.

"Leave them be," said Fisher, content that they had done the very best they could. "By the time we reach Humbie House, it wouldn't surprise me if that marvellous covering hasn't accomplished all the healing they need!"

CHAPTER 26
NIGHT AT THE RUMOUR MILL

Slowly, steadily, dozens of Rescue Capsules from the city of Aletheia formed a precise circle above the Rumour Mill. Below, the Meddlers were trying to regain order. The golden card still burned so brightly that it cast a spotlight over the stark ruin, and, besides this, the capsules had also turned on bright lights – searching, probing, uncovering all of the activities of that ghastly place.

There was a dreadful din. The higher ranks of Meddlers were ordering their subordinates – who were panicking and beginning to fight among themselves. Some were trying to flee, but by now Private PeaceBe and all of the Rescuers from Capsules First, Second, and Third John had dropped to the ground and encircled the Rumour Mill. They lit great beacons of light and drove the alarmed Meddlers back into their unprotected headquarters. Bourne Faithful was in charge of these relatively few ground forces, linked to them all by a variation of the Silent Speaker system. They were all hand-picked warriors, unwavering despite the evil hordes.

Now the Rescue Capsules were in perfect formation, and silently, steadily, they began to descend on the Rumour Mill. From the midst of the ghostly ruin, a rocket flared, speeding straight for the unprotected underbelly of a capsule. The rocket was white and vaporous and streaming poison. In that split second, Bourne ordered, "Sergeant Lowly, neutralise."

Sergeant Jewel Lowly stood at the edge of the forest clearing, some distance from Bourne. She had earned her place in the ranks of Bourne's elite because she was the best shot in the Rescuer forces. She immediately released a golden arrow. It took flight, speeding faster than the white poison, unswerving and precisely on target.

BANG!

A collision of golden sparks and grey-white cloud; the Meddlers' rocket was utterly destroyed. But that did not stop others coming. The Meddlers, in one last desperate attempt to protect the home of their meddling, had rallied and were fighting back.

"Fire as needed!" commanded Bourne, and suddenly he was very busy himself.

Arrow after arrow flew from the hands of the encircling Rescuers, resulting in explosion after explosion of white and gold. Jewel Lowly took out the trickier of the Meddlers' rockets. The air was filled with the stench of poison. Bourne's forces were wearing protective masks, but, even so, they were being slowly infiltrated with the Meddlers' filth. The Meddlers released great cauldrons of contamination, hoping to overcome their attackers and make their escape.

Despite the rocket fire, the Rescue Capsules continued their slow, steady descent, and only now was their purpose visible. Through the poisonous white vapour, a layer of spectacular beauty was slowly enclosing the Meddlers, glimmering and shining like a thousand radiant diamonds. Hoarse cries of horror and consternation rang through the ranks. In desperation, the Meddlers loosed all their remaining white rockets at the descending barrier – but nothing would penetrate the glorious covering of thousands of supplications of the Christians of Aletheia.

Meddlers of all sorts and colours began to rush madly at the Rescuers in their positions on the ground at the edge of the forest. Inevitably, some got away. There was no way the limited ground forces could contain them all.

But the vast majority of the wicked creatures had taken refuge in the hollow ruin, in the middle of their headquarters, perhaps hoping that even yet their leaders and their chosen weapon of poison would save them. Their curses and howls and shrieks and raucous cries rang far and wide as the Rescue Capsules at last extended their long legs and gingerly touched down amongst the tombstones. Dozens of Rescuers rushed from the capsules and joined with the ground forces, forming a human perimeter around the edge of the Rumour Mill. The few Meddlers who made it that far never escaped those fierce, determined warriors. The rest were gasping for air, slowly suffocating under the covering of patient love and prayer and supplication that they could not possibly survive beneath.

Their air was poison; they had no ability to breathe the pure fragrance of love.

Henrietta and Josie forgot their aches and pains as they witnessed the battle at the Rumour Mill. Once the forces from Aletheia had landed, when the dazzlingly beautiful covering had settled on the entire extent of the Rumour Mill, their own capsule touched down safely within the precincts, on a level spot which was peppered with ancient gravestones.

Dawn was streaking across the sky. Since there was no one to forbid them, the girls climbed down from the Rescue Capsule. The utter stillness and peace around them was all the permission they needed. There was no foe here; there was unlikely to be any creature of Err within a mile of this extraordinary protection. For a brief space of time, this hollow ruin, with its surrounding graveyard, almost had the feeling of Aletheia about it.

They walked among the Rescuers who were picking through the rubble of the work of the Meddlers. There was not much left to see. There were no dead bodies to rot and decay; there was no evidence of the great victory which had been won that night. Thousands upon thousands of Meddlers had dissolved under the power of the covering of Truth; it left no trace of decay behind.

But there was some evidence being carefully bagged and labelled by Rescuers. Pieces of parchment, odd bits of printing machines, loose letters and numbers, printed bank notes, wheels and cogs, quills and ink: Josie was fascinated at this insight into the news-making, money-making, corrupt machine of the Meddlers. She and Henrietta saw Bourne with his Mission Detector, recording images for the managers back in Aletheia to examine. Dr Pentone in particular had been most exact about what he wanted to analyse. Bourne lifted his hand in greeting to the girls. They hardly knew when it happened, but in the pure, fresh, radiance of the covering of Aletheia, they revived; injuries began to heal; Henrietta no longer limped.

Before they returned to the Rescue Capsule for the journey home, Henrietta tried to capture some of the glittering strands of the unfathomable weavings of prayer which had settled on the ground. She reached for the sparkling strand caressing the top of that gravestone, but it vanished when she touched it: for those nestling diamonds, like stones on the ground, but they slipped through her fingers. The covering was fading away. She sighed. "I just wanted some to keep, to remind me…"

"It was made for a special purpose," remarked Private PeaceBe, who was close by, and who was wonderfully cheerful after such an astounding victory.

Henrietta looked regretfully at the last of the glorious threads, now vanishing as the light of morning increased in the sky.

Josie took her arm. She also surveyed the ground around her, catching a last glimpse of the wonderful workings of love. "Come, Henry," she said softly, "I'm afraid we'll have to leave it. I don't think this particular prayer offering belongs anywhere else."

CHAPTER 27
MORNING LIGHT

Governor Genie sat in her spacious office. Her fingers nervously drummed her desk. Tap, tap, tap. She shifted in her chair, uncomfortable despite the soft leather and cushions. Tap, tap, tap went her fingers on the desk. If she had dared, she would have gone out into the darkness, into the mist shrouded parklands which surrounded the government headquarters.

But she did not dare. There was nowhere to hide. For the first time she feared the darkness. For the first time she wished she knew more of the light.

Her eyes were riveted apprehensively on the small, tatty cupboard squashed into the corner of her office. Tap, tap, tap went her fingers on the desk. Was no news good news? Tap, tap, tap. Any moment now…

Without warning, the cupboard door crashed open. A small creature with blue stockings on spindly legs slammed rudely into the room. It aimed straight for her desk and reached it before she could draw a startled breath or prepare an opening statement.

"*Betrayed!*" shrieked the creature. "*Betrayed!*"

The worst had happened.

"S-Sir-M-Meddle..." She was actually stammering! She was the elected Governor of the entire land of Err, and she was stammering in front of a creature so small she should have been able to overcome him with one strong swipe. He might be the leader of the feared Meddlers; he might be faster than lightening; he might be without thought or feeling apart from cruelty and destruction. But he was still far smaller, and surely less powerful than she. The Governor tried to pull herself together.

"There w-will be a full inquiry..." It was standard government language, but it didn't appease Sir-Meddle in the least.

Enraged, he tore documents from neat piles on her desk and shredded them in his strong, needle-sharp fingers. They filled the air like ungainly snowflakes and fell in rough heaps on the floor. He splashed ink, stamped on pens, threw paperweights, smashed a vase, destroyed flowers with razor sharp teeth, scribbled on the portraits of governors hung on the walls, tore off strips of the expensive wallpaper she had been so proud of, ripped the leather couch with his awful pointed nails. He was a frantic, terrifying blaze of whirring wings, vicious teeth, and dreadful fury.

"There was really nothing we could do..."

"*You* betrayed us! *You!*" screamed Sir-Meddle. "We are destroyed! The Aletheians' poison! *Your* guards didn't stop it! Pride failed! You let them find us! You didn't stop them! You! You! YOU!"

"I will ensure Pride will pay…"

"*You* will pay!"

"We can help…"

"We will rise again without *you*!"

"How?" For a fleeting moment, she had enjoyed the thought that this evil creature might no longer plague her. She could, even now, cover up this latest disaster; she could bribe the city of Pride to silence – but for Sir-Meddle.

"We will move here," Sir-Meddle gestured disdainfully at the government building around him. "We will feed on meddling here. We will grow strong once more."

Horrified, she stared at the ugly, wrinkled face which was just now so close to her own. His breath was rancid, his miniature fangs dripped venom. It was too terrible to contemplate. The thought of the Meddlers making their home at the Council of Err headquarters, growing strong in their corridors of power…

Sir-Meddle bared his teeth in a cruel snarl. "You will go!" he ordered. "Another will come."

She didn't even protest. All fight was gone. She was powerless against him. Another would indeed come and sit at the Governor's desk that she had occupied with such glorious visions of power and prosperity. Probably Lilotta Mostly would wheedle her way here, change the wallpaper, spend a fortune on furnishings... and then discover the awful secret of the scruffy cupboard in the corner of the office. Very quickly Lilotta, too, would realise she had no power over these dreadful creatures. No one did.

And yet...

There *was* a power which had conquered the Meddlers: the power of light over darkness. It lay in Region 15, in the city of Aletheia. The secrets of the city of Bible Truth could – and would – destroy this hated enemy.

She packed her belongings and Sir-Meddle, savage and wild, banged and raged and shouted.

But she knew what she had to do. She would go to Aletheia.

Morning had coloured the sky a subdued grey when the Rescue Craft approached Humbie House. They had travelled slowly and carefully. In the back of the Craft, the two injured boys slept as soundly as they would have slept even in Aletheia, such was the effect of the Intercessory covering.

In the distance, the gleaming city of Pride was grey and sombre under the subdued light. No longer was a fountain of water gushing high into the sky: instead there was a vast, new lake in the centre of the city, filling the most enormous sinkhole. Just now it was foul and disgusting. But in a short time the frantic City Council would alter the water, and plant a splendid park around the lake, and paint the trees whatever colour was in vogue at the time, and add thousands of synthetic flowers, and advertise a marvellous new holiday park – the new centrepiece for the vain city. They would cover up and paste over and try to forget a most regrettable incident. Only the few who acknowledged the Truth would remember the death and decay which was just below the surface.

Other changes took place in both Pride and Resentment that memorable night. The awful cry of the Meddlers had reached far and wide, and plenty of people had disturbed sleep. Resentment would wake up to find that whole societies had been abandoned; several townsfolk moved away, seeking for peace which had eluded them for so long. Some would travel to Aletheia.

Apart from the massive new lake, and the disastrous disappearance of a whole section of the Quarantine Quality Control facility, the city of Pride woke up to more sinkholes than it would ever admit, including the disappearance of whole City Council departments. Vanitors were confused and didn't function well for days. Visitors didn't come and the border guards had very little to do; Ms Hauteur did not get promotion. Some people moved out to seek for the Truth that had so completely eluded them in this place of self-deceit. Some would visit Humbie House (the demolition order for which was permanently lost); they would listen to Fisher and Gladly Meek; some would reach Aletheia.

It would change, of course. Where there were people who allowed and encouraged them, the Meddlers would rise again. But for weeks and months to come, Fisher and Gladly Meek were very busy indeed.

As they reached the open gates of Humbie House, the two sleeping boys stirred, stretched, yawned, and rubbed their eyes. There was no trace of the wounds of the Meddlers. The poison had been replaced by workings of love. Their healing was complete.

"The blanket..." Charlie fingered the strands, suddenly alert, recognising it at once.

Hugo turned and grinned at him. "I mended it, or at least I tried to," he explained. "But I think it did most of the work itself. Good to have you back, Charlie!"

Charlie looked at Ben. Ben was healed too. "Sorry, Ben," Charlie said gruffly. "I think I see now, that if we'd had this protection..." he lifted the patches of the blanket. "Perhaps, if we'd had this all along, we would have been protected from the Meddlers. We might even have been invisible to them!"

"Such things are hard to find out, son," observed Fisher Meek.

"You might be right; some lessons are definitely learned the hard way. But I would focus on the fact that, although this prayer covering was rejected by you once, it was still offered again! And that is surely the most wonderful thing!"

They went into breakfast.

The night was over; darkness was defeated; morning had come.

Love never fails.

EPILOGUE

The first place that Charlie visited on returning to Aletheia was the cross. He had never understood the attraction of the plain cross in the centre of the city. It was the highest point of Aletheia, and it was undoubtedly the place that the Christians thought about and visited the most. But it had never appealed to him: until now. At last he understood! It was the cross that demonstrated the great, unshakable love of God to a world which rejected Him. It was that love which, despite all Charlie had done against God and against the Truth, had reached and found him when he least deserved it. It was because *God is love* that He sent the Lord Jesus to die; in that act God demonstrated His love – for it was when humanity hated Him that Christ died for them.[16]

The first people Charlie went to visit once he was back in Aletheia were perhaps strange choices. First he went to the Recycle Centre, just outside the city boundary. His friend Bob was pleased enough to see him:

"I wondered where you were," he said. "I've been hearing all sorts about the people up there," he gestured towards the city. "I was afraid they'd taken you captive, or that the pollution had got to you!"

What Charlie could tell Bob about the Meddlers' pollution! That pollution was all about the stench of lies; the Truth was the only thing of pure fragrance. Charlie never used to be at a loss for any words, but it was hard trying to explain to Bob his complete turnaround so far as Aletheia was concerned.

"You want to buy *two Bibles!*" exclaimed Bob in disbelief, at the end of his difficult explanation. "After all these years?! Seems to me you were managing fine without it! And *two!* I shouldn't do myself out of business, but they're really *not* in vogue now, you know, and since you're a friend, I can offer you several other helpful books…"

But Charlie was immovable. There was nothing for him now but the Bible. Leaving Bob looking after him incredulously, he re-entered Aletheia, and, shortly after the border, he detoured to the lone occupant of nearly empty Take-It-Easy Luxury Housing. It was Saturday morning, and, once more, the lonely man was in his silk, patterned dressing gown, holding a large mug of coffee and regarding his beautiful garden disconsolately.

Charlie greeted him cheerfully. "I came back to see you, because I found out why all your friends and neighbours moved close to the cross. And I thought I should come and explain, you see?"

The man didn't seem to see at all. "I'm glad you have your answers, but I'm not sure what that's got to do with me," he said coldly, taking a step back. Suddenly he regretted venturing into his garden this fine spring morning.

"Oh, it's got everything to do with you, alright," Charlie reassured him. "It's got everything to do with everyone in the world…!"

"Listen, young man," the man interrupted haughtily, "I didn't ask you to come here…"

"Oh, it's no problem!" Charlie assured him. "And I had to come; you see, I bought you a gift!"

The man was feeling very helpless in the face of this unlooked for and unwanted generosity. "I really don't think…"

Charlie thrust the spare Bible he had purchased from Bob at the rich man. "It's all in there," he said. "I never knew it before, but all the answers *really are* in there! And it's *all true*! You can read about how important the cross is, because that's where God demonstrated His love when He sent the Lord Jesus to die, and you'll see why all the others ended up moving there, to be close to the Truth of all that God has done…"

It was unfortunate that Charlie, in his enthusiasm, had thrust the Bible into the hand which also held the coffee. The result was a dark stain on the immaculate silk dressing gown, and the man's face glowed red with annoyance.

"Sorry about the coffee!" said Charlie quickly. "It's just as well you aren't properly dressed yet, isn't it?" he added comfortingly. But his remark didn't appear to soothe the man's wounded feelings at all.

He was sent packing with angry words ringing in his ears. As he made his way back to the centre of Aletheia, high on the hill above the lonely rich man, he thought about how unreasonable and provoking and awful his own behaviour had been. And yet, despite that, his friends had acted out love in the most remarkable way. They had helped to clear his muddled mind of the poison of the Meddlers' lies; through his friends he had undoubtedly been helped to see the love of God.

So now it was his turn. He must act in love towards Bob at the Recycle Centre, and the angry rich man too. He must bear their jibes and rejection with patience; he must return injury with kindness; he must never envy or begrudge the rich man's possessions: he must boast only about what the Lord Jesus has done; he must not be rude or selfish or angry, no matter how they behaved towards him: instead he must forget and keep no account of any wrong done to himself; he must never again be entertained by Bob's gossip about other people – he must not rejoice in sin. He must instead learn to bear all things – to throw a covering over the faults of others and not expose weaknesses to ridicule; he must remember that the Lord Jesus can cleanse every sin and wrong; he must endure – and keep acting out love – and never give up.

Of course, he couldn't do it on his own or he would fail. But the same God Who loved him, had also promised never to leave him or forsake him.[25] And when showing love was hard or seemed to fail, God wouldn't leave him to deal with it alone.

God had shown such great love to him; He had shown people *how* to love.

And love never fails.

Weary and battered from the fight, Bourne Faithful slowly climbed the last few steps to the room with the golden door. When the clear up from Operation Grey was complete, he promised himself a holiday; he wondered, as he sometimes did, about travelling to the strangely named place where those remarkable boys, Jack Merryweather and Timmy Trial,[26] had their home. He would like to see it sometime. But first some tasks must be completed, and here, in the very highest precincts of the Prayer Academy, was one of great importance. He placed his Bible onto the book-shaped indentation carved delicately on the golden door. There was a soft click. He entered the room.

"Well, well," said little old Mrs Pentone, the clever mother of the great Dr Pentone. She looked up from her work station where she was carefully laying gold leaf onto dazzling golden cards. "Well, well, if it isn't our very own Lieutenant safely returned from the battle!"

From a dozen other older men and women, Bourne was met with a chorus of similar comments and warm greetings and enquiries as to the fight. They all knew the results by now, but there was nothing like firsthand information from one of their favourite warriors.

Bourne scanned the worn and wrinkled and weary faces. They were all engaged in tasks of the most incredible intricacy and wonderful beauty. They all worked together on each golden card they produced: refining the gold, carving verses from the Bible, adding gold leaf and hidden details which none other than themselves ever knew about. As an experienced warrior, Bourne knew the value of what they produced, and he knew that four teenagers did too – although they had never seen the patient labour of prayer which went into each precious card.

"I've come to thank you for the four prayer cards you refined for me, for the members of Operation Grey."

Every member of the specialist prayer group gathered in that hidden room knew the names of the four members of Operation Grey by heart. They had, after all, made their golden cards especially for them, and had prayed for them ever since. Bourne observed the eager, lined faces as they listened to him recounting the use of each card –

always used on account of someone else – and the miraculous results. These here, *these* were the ones who had really fought the battle – albeit behind the lines where no one would ever know all they had done. There was a time they had fought for him too: the time he had acquired the scar on his face; he knew they would go on fighting for him yet.

"Just as it should be," said Mrs Pentone, when he finished his account. "We have a great God who does above and beyond what we ask or think!"

Mrs De Voté, who worked in this special room when time allowed, smiled at the young warrior. "Love never fails!" she said.

Of course, Bourne knew why love would never fail:

Because God Himself is love.[20]

REFERENCES

Unless otherwise stated, all Bible references are taken from the New King James Version of the Bible.

1. [References on pages 18, 19, 20, 43, 99, 101, 104] You can read about this in The Defenders of Aletheia, Aletheia Adventure Series Book 5.

2. [References on pages 19, 96] Someone becomes a Christian when they trust the Lord Jesus, and have therefore been saved from the punishment they deserve for their sins. There are many verses in the Bible which explain how you become a Christian (how you are saved). For example,

Acts 16:31:
"Believe on the Lord Jesus Christ, and you will be saved."

John 3:16:
"For God so loved the world that He gave His only begotten Son, that whoever believes in Him should not perish but have everlasting life."

260 The Rumour Mill

3. [References on pages 54 (2), 62, 80, 89, 129, 144, 154, 175, 195, 203, 211] The Bible talks about Christians putting on the 'armour of God'. This is explained in

    Ephesians 6:10-18:

    "Finally, my brethren, be strong in the Lord and in the power of His might.

    Put on the whole armour of God, that you may be able to stand against the wiles of the devil. For we do not wrestle against flesh and blood, but against principalities, against powers, against the rulers of the darkness of this age, against spiritual hosts of wickedness in the heavenly places. Therefore take up the whole armour of God, that you may be able to withstand in the evil day, and having done all, to stand.

    Stand therefore, having girded your waist with truth, having put on the breastplate of righteousness, and having shod your feet with the preparation of the gospel of peace; above all, taking the shield of faith with which you will be able to quench all the fiery darts of the wicked one. And take the helmet of salvation, and the sword of the Spirit, which is the word of God; praying always with all prayer and supplication in the Spirit…"

4. [References on pages 82] This is a reference to a verse which

explains how the Bible can act as a light to show us the way.

Psalm 119:105:

"Your word is a lamp to my feet

And a light to my path."

[This doesn't mean that the Bible is a literal light; the verse is saying that the Word of God will be our guide through life if we believe what it says.]

5. [References on pages 89, 122, 136, 182] The Bible makes it clear that there is no sin – no wrong – that the Lord Jesus can't cleanse us from if we trust in Him. For example,

1 John 1:7:

"And the blood of Jesus Christ His [God's] Son cleanses us from all sin."

1 John 1:9:

"If we confess our sins, He is faithful and just to forgive us our sins and to cleanse us from all unrighteousness."

6. [References on pages 91, 105] You can read about this in The Mustardseeds, Aletheia Adventure Series Book 4.

7. [References on pages 101, 116] You can read about this in The Purple Storm, Aletheia Adventure Series Book 2.

8. [Reference on page 103] This is a reference to

Ephesians 6:18:

"Praying always with all prayer and supplication in the Spirit, being watchful to this end with all perseverance and supplication for all the saints."

9. [References on pages 103, 174] This is a reference to

Philippians 4:6-7:

"Be anxious for nothing, but in everything by prayer and supplication, with thanksgiving, let your requests be made known to God; and the peace of God, which surpasses all understanding, will guard your hearts and minds through Christ Jesus."

10. [Reference on page 106] This is a reference to

Galatians 6:2:

"Bear one another's burdens, and so fulfill the law of Christ."

11. [References on pages 115, 155] This quote is from a passage in

the Bible, 1 Corinthians chapter 13, which describes the actions of love.

1 Corinthians 13:4-8:

"Love suffers long and is kind; love does not envy; love does not parade itself, is not puffed up; does not behave rudely, does not seek its own, is not provoked, thinks no evil; does not rejoice in iniquity, but rejoices in the truth; bears all things, believes all things, hopes all things, endures all things. Love never fails."

You can read these same verses in the International Children's Bible which phrases them slightly differently:

"Love is patient and kind. Love is not jealous, it does not boast, and it is not proud. Love is not rude, is not selfish, and does not become angry easily. Love does not remember wrongs done against it. Love is not happy with evil, but is happy with the truth. Love patiently accepts all things. It always trusts, always hopes, and always continues strong. Love never ends."

12. [Reference on page 117] There are verses in the Bible which explain that God will answer prayer when we ask something in keeping with His will. (Since the Bible is the Word of God, God's will is always in keeping with the Bible). For example,

John 14:13:

"And whatever you ask in My name, that I will do."

1 John 5:14:

"If we ask anything according to His [God's] will, He hears us."

13. [References on pages 128, 206] You can read about this in The Broken Journey, Aletheia Adventure Series Book 3.

14. [Reference on page 132] Genesis chapter 3 in the Bible explains how sin entered into the world when Adam and Eve disobeyed God in the Garden of Eden. They ate of fruit which God had forbidden, because they wanted to be wise like God. Their pride – their desire to be as powerful as God – led to the fall of mankind.

15. [Reference on page 133] The Bible teaches that there is no one who is good and who can meet God's standards. That is why we need to trust in the Lord Jesus to be made right with God. A verse about this is

Romans 3:10-12:

"As it is written:

'There is none righteous, no, not one;

There is none who understands;

There is none who seeks after God.

They have all turned aside;

They have together become unprofitable;

There is none who does good, no, not one.'"

16. [References on pages 135, 213, 252] This is a reference to
Romans 5:8:

"God demonstrates His own love toward us, in that while we were still sinners, Christ died for us."

17. [References on pages 162, 209] This is a reference to
Proverbs 16:18:

"Pride goes before destruction,

And a haughty spirit before a fall."

18. [References on pages 196, 217] The Bible teaches that the Lord Jesus is the only way people can be right with God. The Lord Jesus said that He was the way back to God. He is the only truth.
John 14:6:

"Jesus said to him, 'I am the way, the truth, and the life. No one comes to the Father except through Me.'"

19. [References on pages 201, 212] This is a reference to

1 John 4:9-10:

"In this the love of God was manifested toward us, that God has sent His only begotten Son into the world, that we might live through Him. In this is love, not that we loved God, but that He loved us and sent His Son to be the propitiation for our sins."

You can read these same verses in the International Children's Bible which phrases them slightly differently:

"This is how God showed his love to us: he sent his only Son into the world to give us life through him. True love is God's love for us, not our love for God. God sent his Son to be the way to take away our sins."

20. [References on pages 213, 258] The Bible teaches that God is love.

1 John 4:16:

"And we have known and believed the love that God has for us. God is love, and he who abides in love abides in God, and God in him."

21. [Reference on page 213] The Bible is full of reasons why God

should be trusted. The Bible often tells us that God does not change, nor will He fail us. For example,

Malachi 3:6:

"For I am the Lord, I do not change."

Deuteronomy 31:6:

"Be strong and of good courage, do not fear nor be afraid of them; for the Lord your God, He is the One who goes with you. He will not leave you nor forsake you."

22. [Reference on page 213] 'Sin' is the Bible name for all the wrong things that everyone has done. The Bible teaches that everyone has sinned against God – none of us can meet His standards.

Romans 3:23:

"For all have sinned and fall short of the glory of God."

23. [Reference on page 213] The Bible describes the Lord Jesus as the mediator who can bring people back to God.

1 Timothy 2:5:

"For there is one God and one Mediator between God and men, the Man Christ Jesus."

[Note that 'men' here means all people.]

24. [Reference on page 213] The Bible teaches that the sacrifice of the Lord Jesus means that, if we trust in Him, we are reconciled [brought back] to God.

Romans 5:11:

"We also rejoice in God through our Lord Jesus Christ, through whom we have now received the reconciliation."

25. [Reference on page 256] This is a reference to

Hebrews 13:5:

"For He Himself has said, 'I will never leave you nor forsake you.' So we may boldly say:

'The Lord is my helper;

I will not fear.

What can man do to me?'"

26. [Reference on page 256] Jack Merryweather and Timmy Trial feature in other Aletheia Adventure books. You can read about them in books 1, 3, 4, and 5 of the series.